A BASIC
VOCABULARY
american sign language
for parents and children

INTRODUCTION BY: DR. URSULA BELLUGI

BY TERRENCE J. O'ROURKE

ILLUSTRATED BY:

FRANK ALLEN PAUL

RESEARCH ILLUSTRATOR
THE SALK INSTITUTE
LA JOLLA, CALIFORNIA

SIGN MODEL-CONSULTANTS:

GIL EASTMAN   ELLA LENTZ   DOROTHY MILES

CARLENE PEDERSEN   KEN PEDERSEN   JANE WILK

A special thanks to the two deaf children that
posed with Ken and Carlene Pedersen for our book cover design.

FLAVIA FLEISCHER/DAUGHTER OF LARRY AND VERA FLEISCHER
AMERICO PEDERSEN/SON OF MELVIN AND ESTHER PEDERSEN

Printed in United States of America

© 1978, T. J. PUBLISHERS, INC.
  8805 Arliss Street
  Silver Spring, Maryland 20901

ISBN #0-932666-00-0
Library of Congress Catalog No.: 78-63151

DEDICATION

To all children of deaf parents, deaf and hearing.

FOREWORD

The most prevalent handicapping factor of deafness arises from its interference with communication. Difficulties in the deaf child's language growth, social interaction and academic development originate from that source. It is basic that you as a parent develop a standard means to communicate with your child.

Communication is a basic human right. It is the means by which we learn and relate to the larger society of which we are a part. Learning to communicate with your child so that all can be understood is essential for total family involvement.

Developing fluency in sign language takes time. The effort is gratifying and worthwhile, but you must dedicate yourself to the effort.

For the many parents who wish to improve communication with their child, this book is a practical approach to communication focusing on helping parents develop a practical vocabulary of sign language.

August, 1978

Lavenia A. Faison
Executive Director
International Association
    of Parents of the Deaf

TABLE OF CONTENTS

INTRODUCTION

This is an important and timely book, created specifically for parents of deaf children. This book will provide you with tools which enable your child's mind to blossom.

The processes by which young pre-school hearing children acquire their native language has been the focus of basic research over the past two decades. Researchers in language acquisition have made a rather surprising discovery. They have found that children play a very active role in the acquisition process itself. All over the world, children master the complex rules of the language to which they are exposed in a very short time. They do so generally without specific training in grammatical rules, without instruction in the formation of tenses, plurals, embeddings, and so forth, and without being constantly corrected or taught. Children, moreover, apparently do not learn specifically by imitating what they hear; in fact, their imitations often show characteristic error patterns which give clues to their own construction rules.

Some time between the ages of eighteen months and five years, children extract from speech they hear around them a set of construction rules that later enable them to produce indefinitely numerous, new sentences that will be correctly understood in their language community. As Roger Brown puts it, "It looks as if child speech is, in some respect, the same everywhere in the world; as if it has some universal properties, as if there were some universal stages of development." Curiously, one of the most significant sources of evidence that children are indeed learning construction rules, and not merely imitating or memorizing what they hear, is in the typical kinds of "mistakes" they make—that is, mistakes from the point of view of the adult language. Children produce "goed" instead of "went"; "tooths" instead of "teeth", and questions like "Is it was a snake?" or "Why I can't do that?" Researchers in many countries have found that children invent their own rules at relatively predictable stages, and then spontaneously change to more adult forms. Such inventions are common in the language acquisition process. When they are consistently made at a particular stage, they reveal not that the child is "wrong" and needs correcting, but that he is extracting general rules of construction from the language around him, and is playing a very active role in the language acquisition process. He is reconstructing language just as actively as he is practicing and perfecting his skills at locomotion at comparable stages, first crawling, pulling himself up, then toddling and finally walking.

But now, consider the child who is born deaf. He does not have access to spoken language input, for he is insulated, isolated from the spoken language that flows around him. Although the deaf child has the same desire to communicate as all children, he is effectively cut off from an auditory means of developing his natural language learning capacity. A deaf child of hearing parents may grow up in just such an isolated situation.

The alternative for deaf children which makes full use of a child's language learning abilities is through a mode of communication—a language—which has developed spontaneously in the absence of hearing among deaf people. This language is American Sign Language. It has developed in the hands and for the eyes. Researchers have found, rather to their surprise, that the sign language of the deaf is a fully developed language, with a complex grammar, with its own rules of construction, and its own way of incorporating semantic information into the basic sign. Thus, one can provide language for deaf children in a modality that does not depend on hearing. It is a language specifically suited to the visual mode.

Studies of deaf children of deaf parents show that, given language input, the language acquisition process in deaf and hearing children is essentially comparable. It is as if there is an underlying maturational timetable, and language emerges at the same rate and in the same stages, whether the input is spoken language or sign language. Moreover, deaf children learning sign language as a native language from their deaf parents also play an active role in the process just as do hearing children. They see, not just the instances they are exposed to, but the construction rules of the language. As their errors reveal, they extract the basic regularities of the language.

But most significantly, such deaf children have a full social role in the family, without drilling or specific concentrated language instruction, without focusing on language itself, but rather through focusing on the extended communication which language permits. There is a way to communicate about past and future, about what is not present, and what could happen, to develop fantasies and stories; for most of all, language is a vehicle for thought and for the child's mind to develop. Such a vehicle also permits the child to develop his own personality, his own self, to reconstruct the world for himself. The child develops, in this way, not only language, but more important, a sense of himself, his relation to the family, and to the world.

This book, then, was developed to fill a basic need: to provide a vehicle of communication between hearing parents and their deaf children. It is based on the vocabulary of pre-school children, providing signs for the things that children talk about everywhere. The signs were chosen using a large number of basic word lists, with attention to the vocabulary of young children, and those who model them for you whether born hearing or deaf.

This book provides a means for parents of deaf children to develop ways of communicating directly, freely, openly with their deaf children—ways of explaining things to them, of talking about the past or making plans for the future, of communicating about feelings, wants, needs, intentions, and ideas. Above all, it provides for the possibility of permitting the child's mind to expand and grow at the normal time and in the normal way.

The significance of such tools for communication was impressed on me by a very simple event that occurred during one of our visits to a deaf family. The deaf two year old was signing animatedly to use about her visit with her grandparents. Her favorite doll, lying near her on the table, was in imminent danger of being knocked down by her articulate and excited gestures; her father gently removed the doll to prevent its falling. The child, seeing her favorite toy removed, was startled, and stopped signing and began to cry. A quiet sentence from her father, which explained that he was just holding it temporarily for safe keeping, immediately stilled the impending storm of tears, and the child returned to her story telling with a smile. A very small incident, to be sure. But I wondered what would have happened on this occasion, and on thousands of similar occasions, without that ability to communicate simple messages about intent and about the future. How difficult it must be for someone without the ability to say where it hurts, or what will happen, or what is needed, or to ask what something is called, or what it means, or why the moon seems to follow you at night as you walk.

For language is a tool, a master tool with which all other tools can be created. Language is our way of symbolizing and sharing experience, of passing on knowledge from one generation to the next. Without language, the mind must be forever imprisoned in the immediate unreasoned present; with language, the mind is free to explore past and future.

This book, then, is important as a tool for enabling communication to occur in the first place; for providing for expression of needs, wants, feelings; for providing for the growth of a child's mind and teaching him about the world and his place in it. Such early learning of sign language, lays a foundation for communicating by all kinds of other means, and for forging bridges between human beings, hearing and deaf.

By Dr. Ursula Bellugi, Director
The Laboratory for Language Studies
The Salk Institute for Biological Studies
La Jolla, California

PREFACE

The growing acceptance of the "Total Communication" approach to teaching deaf children has created a need for sign language dictionaries that contain the lexical items used in the daily communication milieu of deaf children. This milieu includes not only interaction among parent and child, and teacher and child, but also between child and child. As with any learning situation, peer interaction plays a very important role. Falberg[1] has suggested that sign language, in its broadest sense, is the only language extant that has been passed down from child to child. Yet those dictionaries presently on the market fail to take advantage not only of this fact, but also of the fact that recent research on American Sign Language (ASL) has clearly defined the formal devices[2] for creating new signs in ASL.

In the rush to develop "language" materials for deaf children, professionals who themselves are unfamiliar with the *language,* have sought to apply the grammatical structure and formal devices for creating new words in English, superimpose them on the language of signs, and label this a "system" for teaching English. Rather than use the *internal* formal devices that are inherent in ASL, most present dictionaries use one *external* mechanism for expansion: borrowing from the dominant language of the surrounding community. This book seeks to emphasize the internal mechanisms that make ASL a unique and vibrant language: derivational processes, syntactic processes, and several kinds of processes for compounding.

No lengthy discourse on the various mechanisms mentioned above is contained within this book. Rather, the selection of lexical items illustrates the natural ways in which the lexicon of ASL is expanded and is expandable.

A manual by Charlotte Baker and Dennis Cokely giving a detailed description of the grammatical devices of ASL and a new ASL text, *A Basic Course in American Sign Language* are presently being prepared and will be published soon by T.J. Enterprises, Inc. These books are recommended for anyone seeking to expand his/her knowledge of ASL beyond the lexical level.

The vocabulary used in this book was selected from a number of basic word lists, including developmental lists from both deaf and hearing children, which were matched for duplication and then pared to approximately 1,000 items. Certain words not found in basic word lists but peculiar to a deaf child's environment (e.g.: hearing aid) were then added.

In many instances, it was necessary to make an arbitrary choice from among several signs that could be described as dialectical, in the same way that *crawfish, crawdad,* and *crayfish* are used in English in different parts of the country to describe the same crustacean. However, the choice, as in the case of the word *corn,* was from among the various natural signs for "corn".

---

[1]Falberg, R.   National Association of the Deaf Communicative Skills Program Advisory Board Meeting. Tucson, Arizona: February, 1971.

[2]Bellugi, U.   Formal Devices for Creating New Signs in ASL. To appear in Wm. Stokoe (Ed.) *Proceedings of the National Symposium on Sign Language Research and Teaching*, Chicago, Illinois. May, 1977.

While borrowing from the dominant language is one of the external mechanisms for expanding the lexicon of signs, through fingerspelling, loan signs, initialized signs, and borrowing from printed symbols, every attempt has been made to include only those "external" signs that, through the test of time, have been assimilated into the language by native users of the language. All of the sign models, with one exception, are themselves native users of ASL; most are children of deaf parents.

It may be useful to note here that the signs are *not* arranged in exact alphabetical order. In many instances, especially in the case of compounds, it was necessary to arrange pages in such a way that the alphabetical sequence had to be discarded. The index, however, follows alphabetical order.

Although it is the belief of the author that the illustrator is the country's number one sign illustrator, the two-dimensional line drawing can never fully depict the three-dimensional nature of signs. For this reason, a notation system on movement has been devised, which includes notation on the noun and verb modulations of listed signs, and of compounds. The notation system is:

$$(V) = \text{verb}$$
$$(N) = \text{noun}$$
$$(DM) = \text{double movement}$$
$$(AM) = \text{alternating movement}$$
$$(W) = \text{fingers wiggle}$$
$$(CC) = \text{compound}$$

While this book was developed primarily as a resource for parents of deaf children, it is also an excellent source for teachers in the "Total Communication" setting, especially those in the pre-school and primary grades. Because the vocabulary was chosen from basic word lists, this book also can be used as a basic text for any beginning class in signs. No teaching units are included, as the book is adaptable to a variety of teaching and learning situations.

As a final word, I would like to acknowledge the valuable assistance of the sign models, and a special indebtedness to Jane Norman Wilk, who assisted in most phases of the development of this book while she was Coordinator of Special Projects for the Communicative Skills Program while on a one-year leave of absence from Gallaudet College during the 1976–77 academic year.

Terrence J. O'Rourke

SIGNS
american sign language

Aa

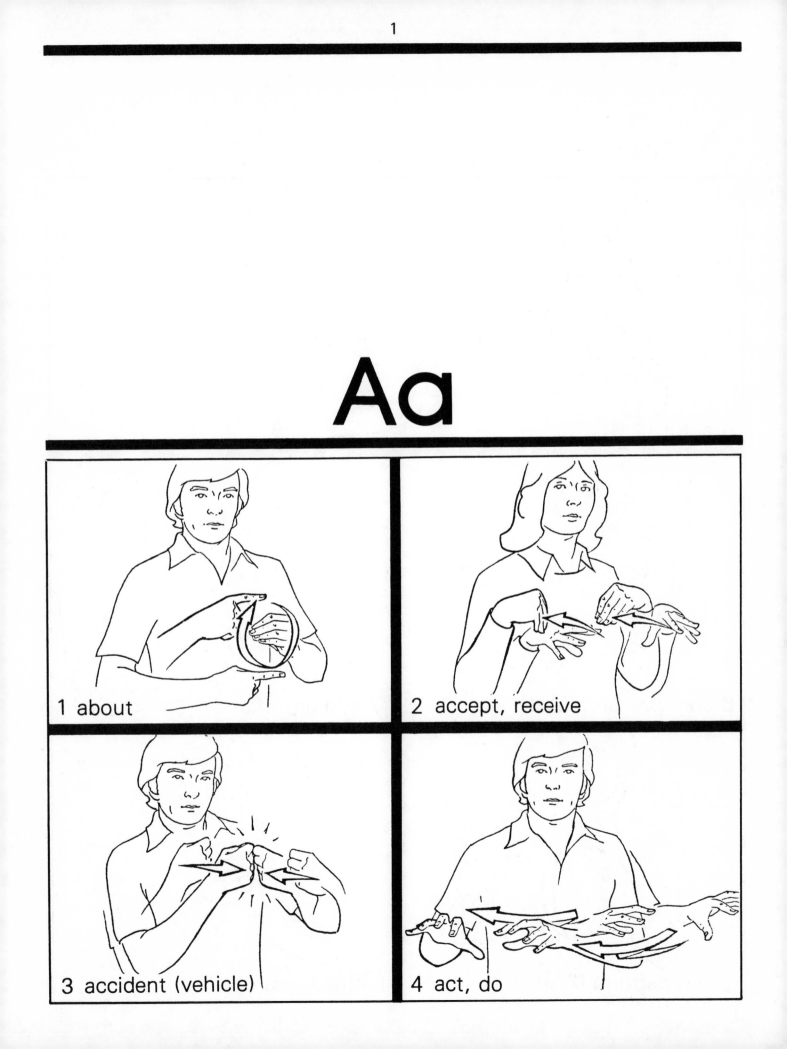

1 about

2 accept, receive

3 accident (vehicle)

4 act, do

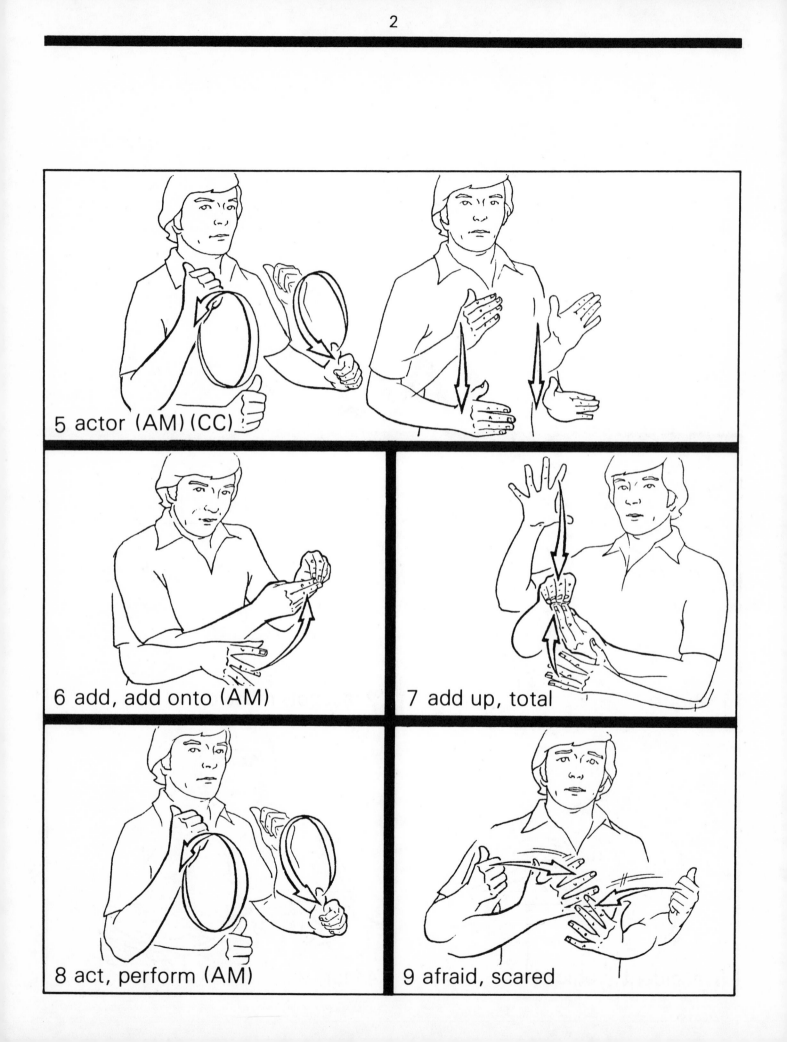

5 actor (AM) (CC)

6 add, add onto (AM)

7 add up, total

8 act, perform (AM)

9 afraid, scared

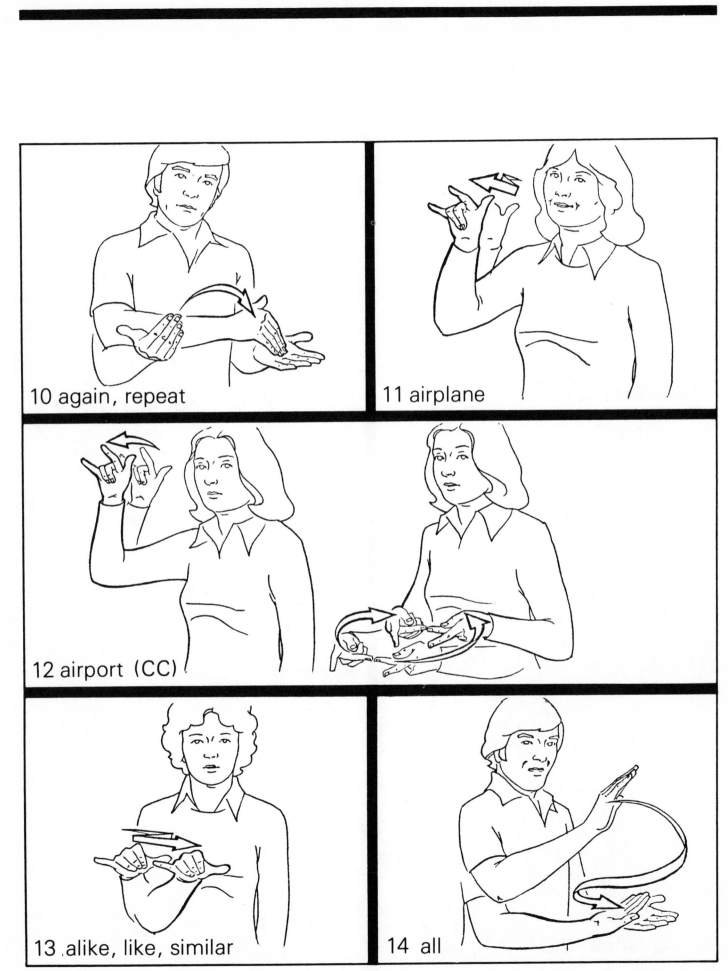

10 again, repeat

11 airplane

12 airport (CC)

13 alike, like, similar

14 all

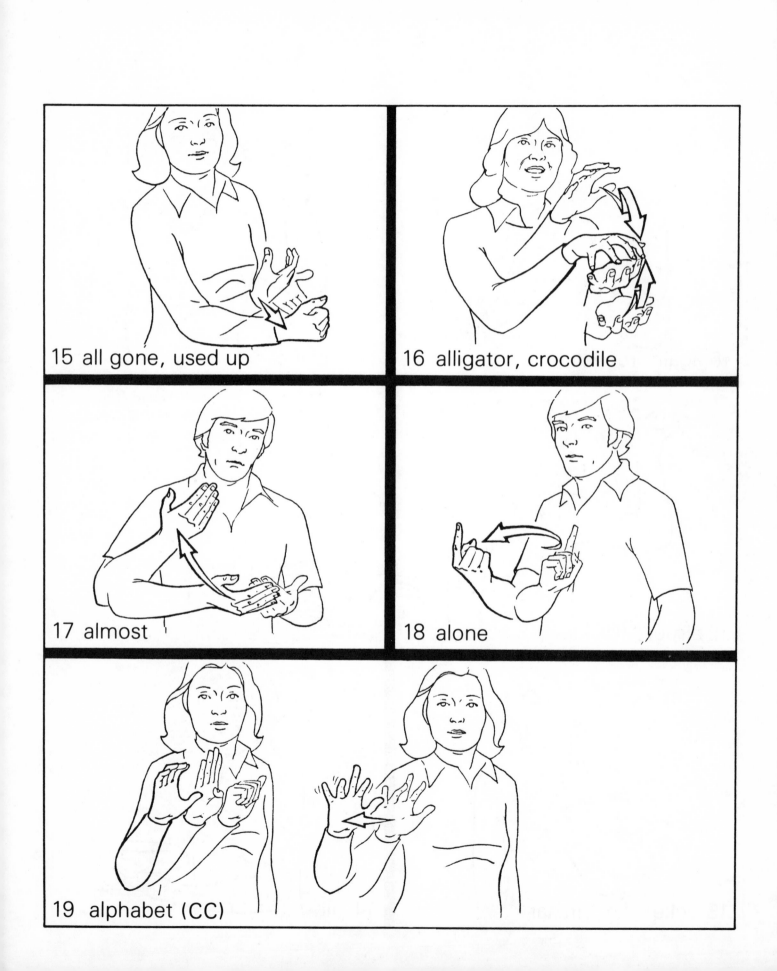

15 all gone, used up

16 alligator, crocodile

17 almost

18 alone

19 alphabet (CC)

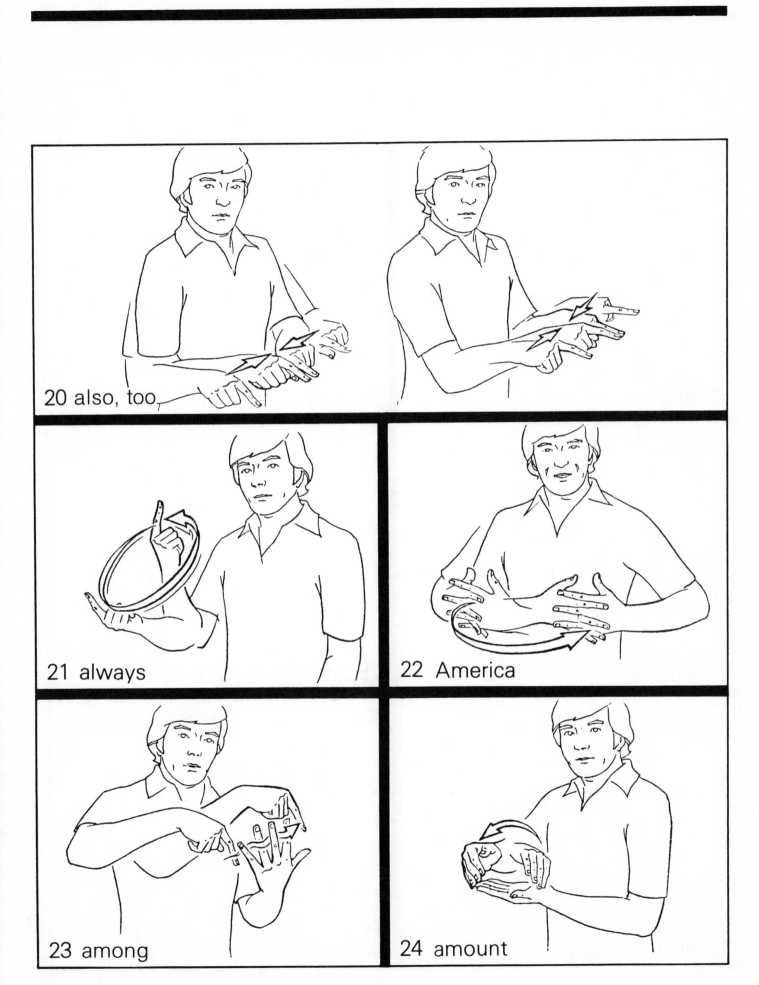

20 also, too

21 always

22 America

23 among

24 amount

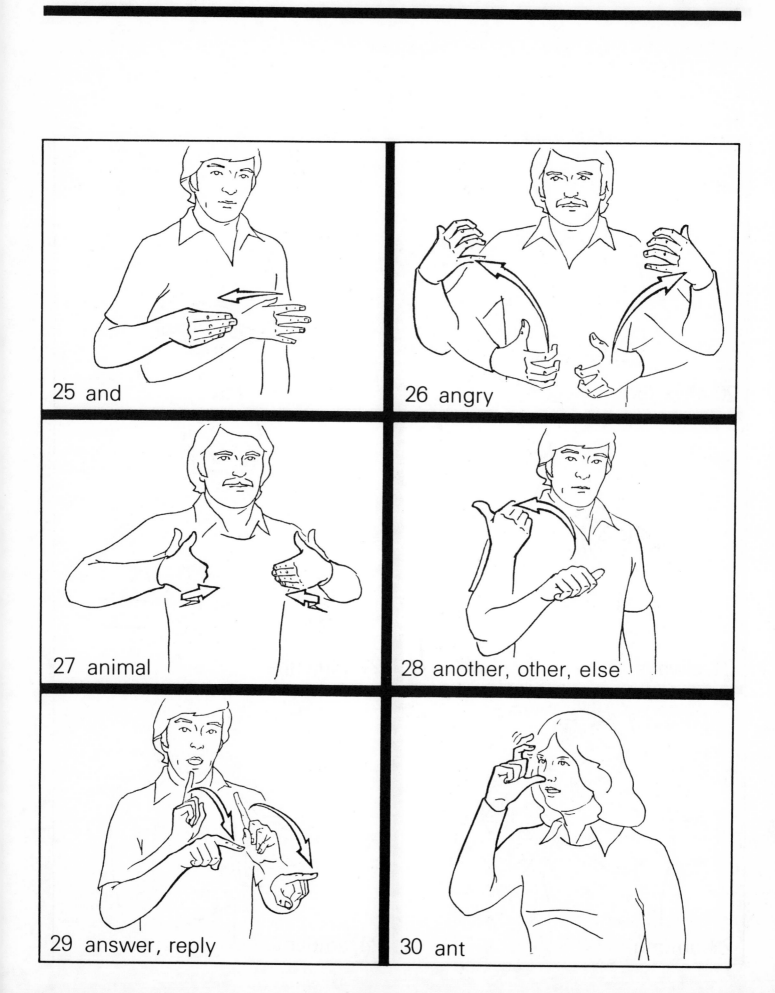

25 and

26 angry

27 animal

28 another, other, else

29 answer, reply

30 ant

31 anything (CC)

32 any

33 appear, seem

34 appear, show up

35 apple

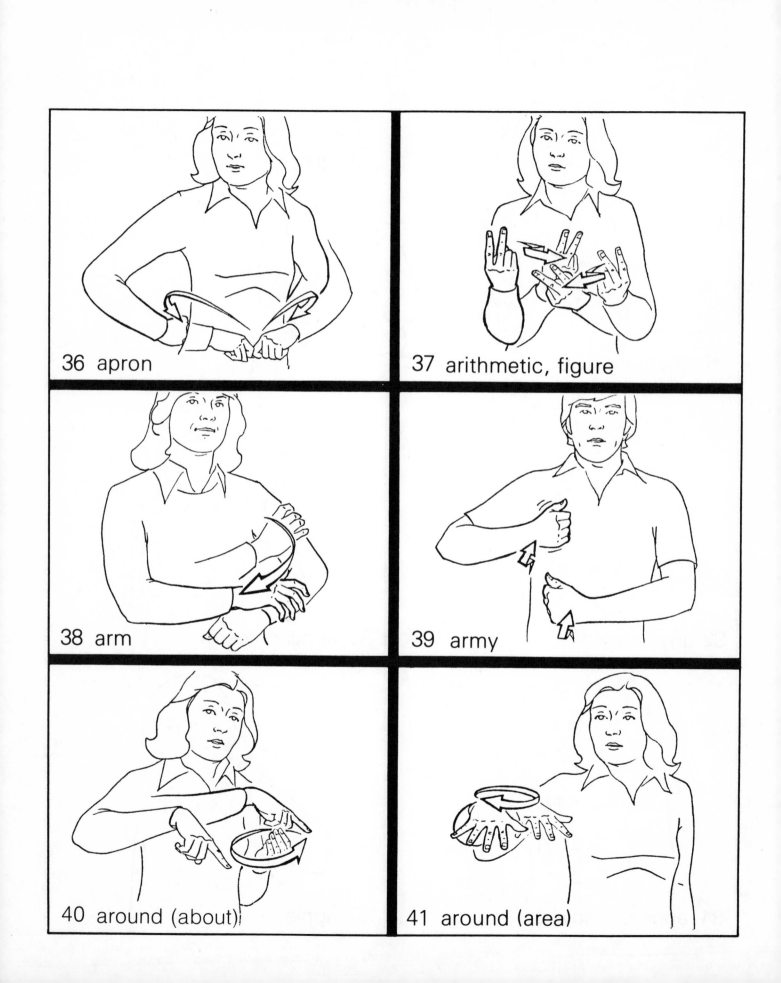

36 apron

37 arithmetic, figure

38 arm

39 army

40 around (about)

41 around (area)

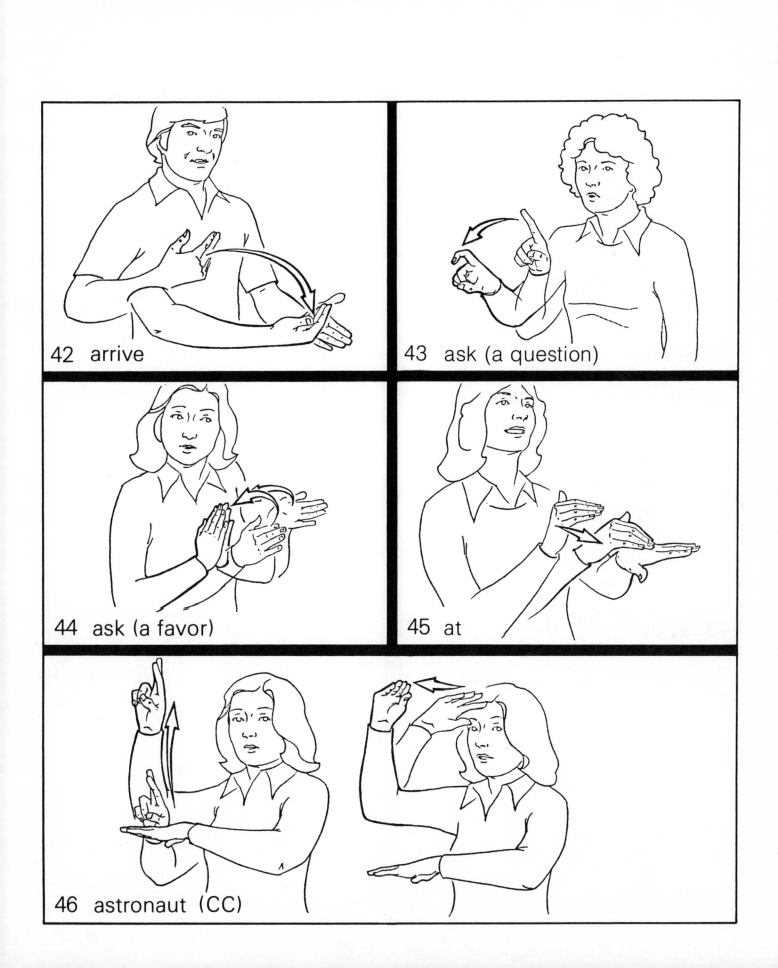

42 arrive

43 ask (a question)

44 ask (a favor)

45 at

46 astronaut (CC)

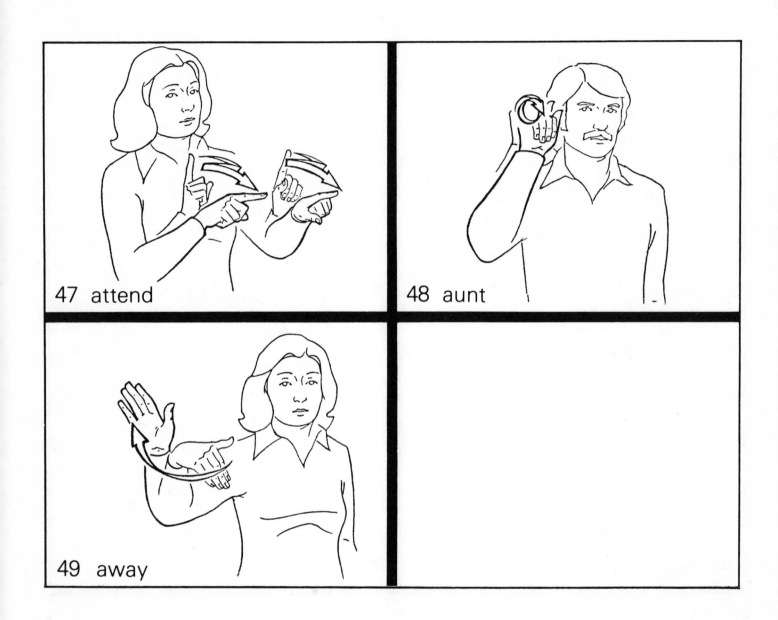

47 attend

48 aunt

49 away

Bb

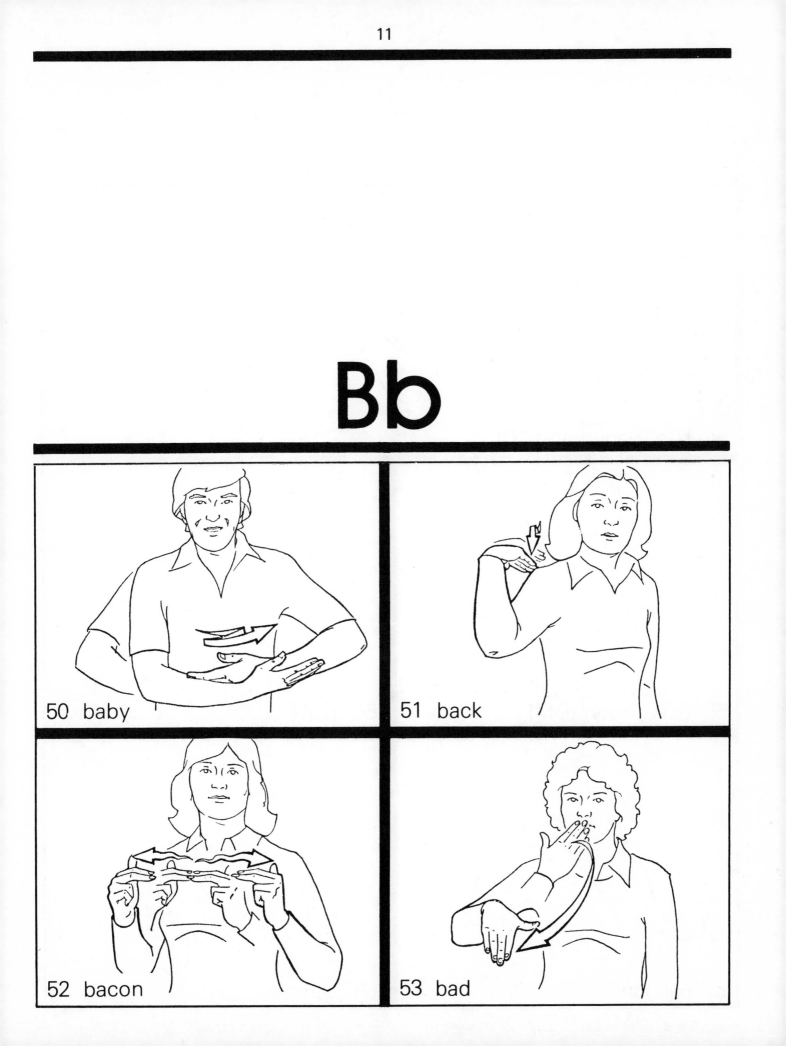

50 baby

51 back

52 bacon

53 bad

54 bag, paperbag (CC)

55 bake, oven (DM)

56 ball

57 balloon

58 banana

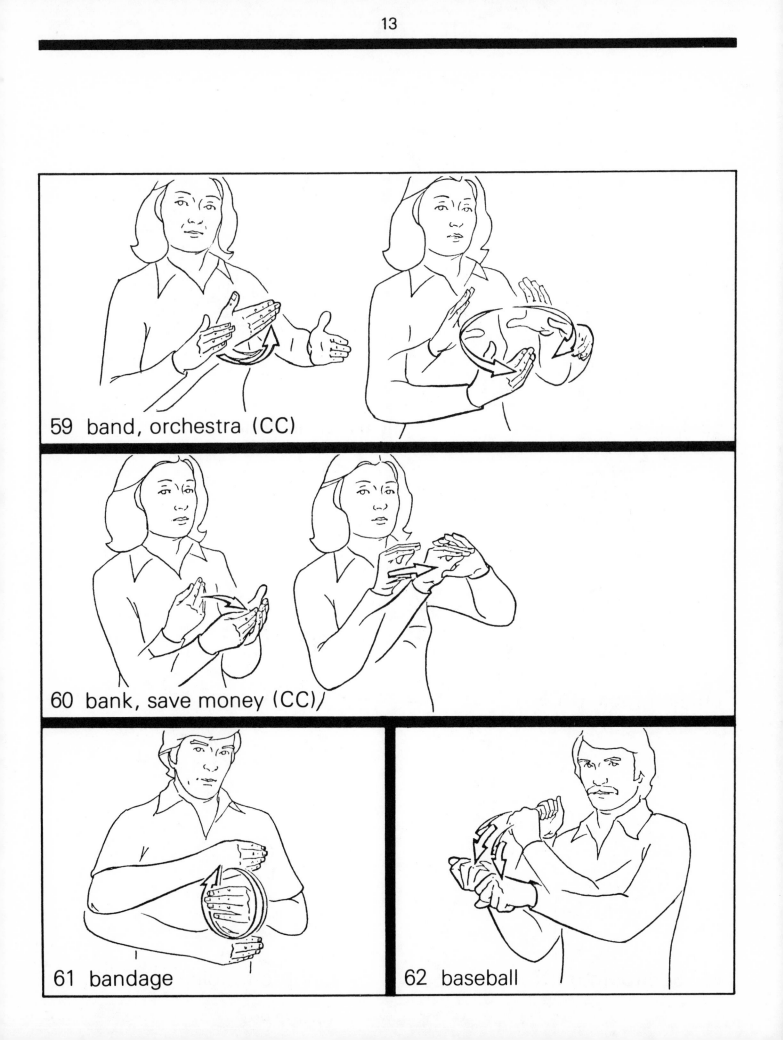

59 band, orchestra (CC)

60 bank, save money (CC)

61 bandage

62 baseball

63 basket

64 basketball

65 bathrobe (CC)

66 bathroom, restroom

67 bathroom, toilet

68 bathtub (CC)

69 bay (CC)

70 beads, necklace

71 bean

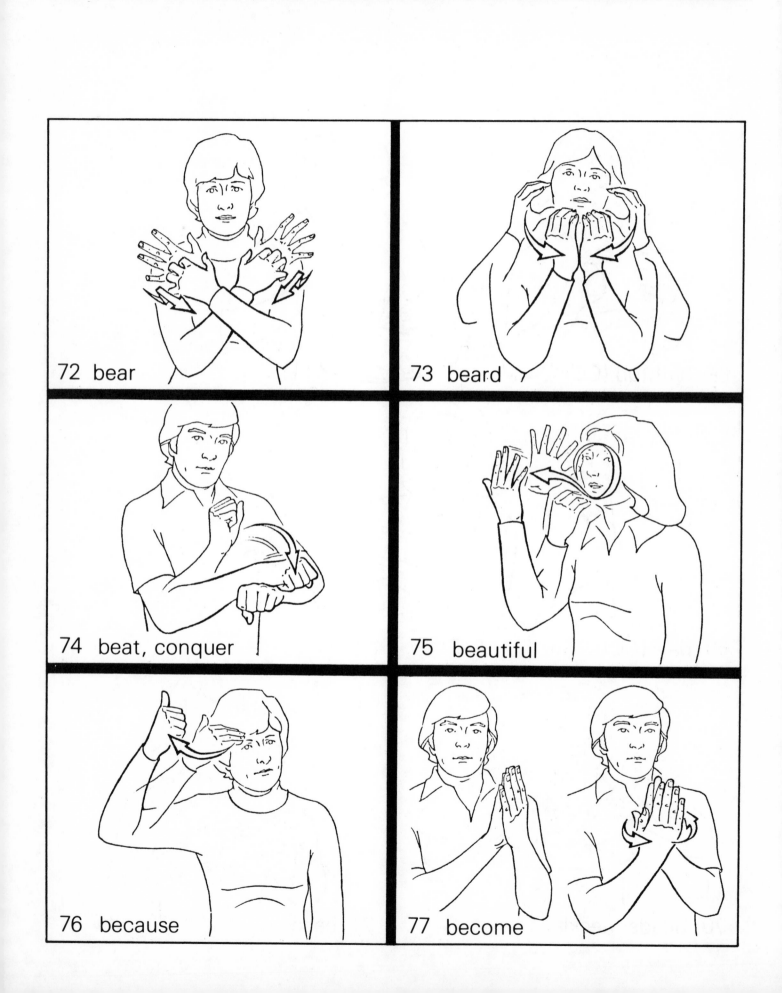

72 bear

73 beard

74 beat, conquer

75 beautiful

76 because

77 become

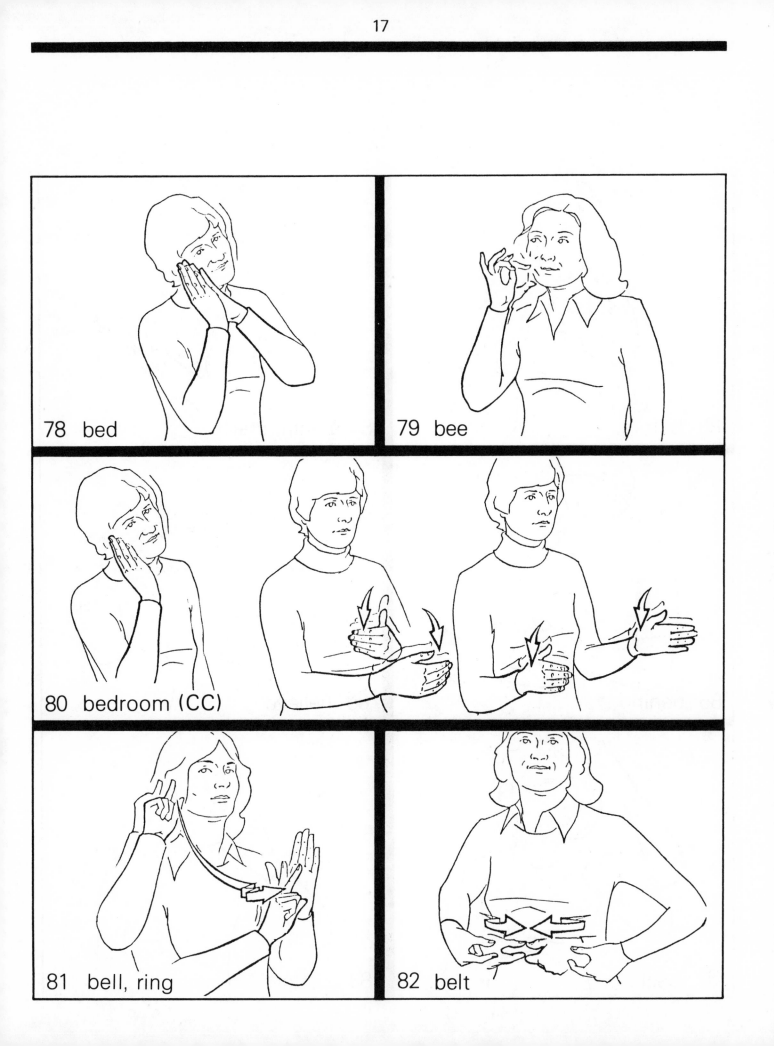

78 bed

79 bee

80 bedroom (CC)

81 bell, ring

82 belt

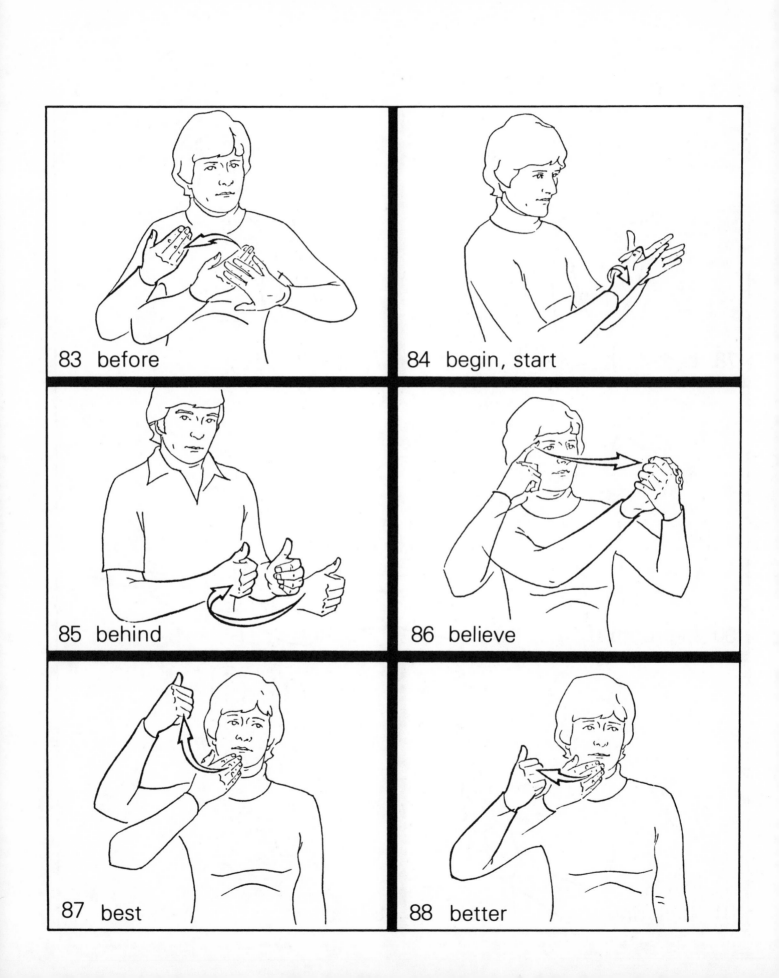

83 before

84 begin, start

85 behind

86 believe

87 best

88 better

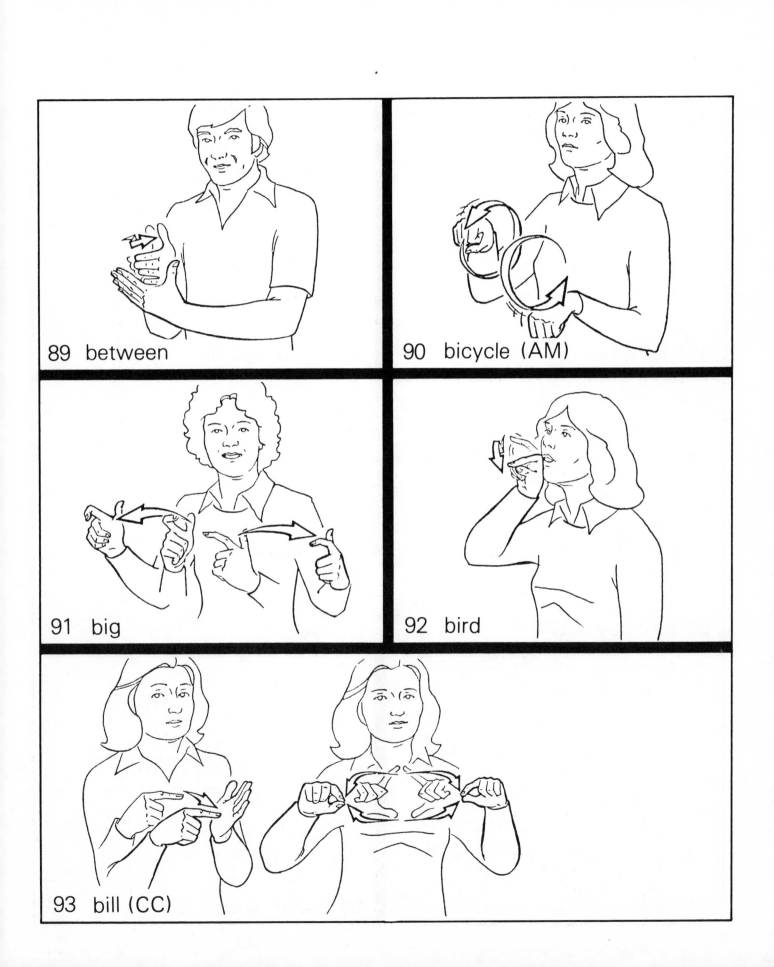

89 between

90 bicycle (AM)

91 big

92 bird

93 bill (CC)

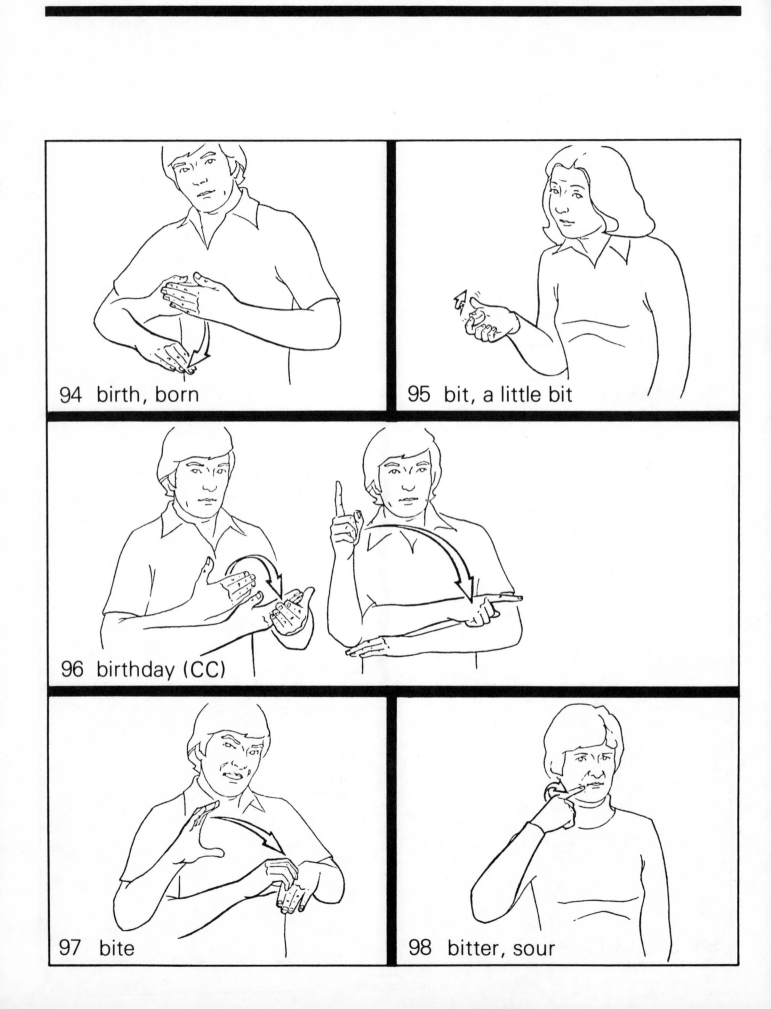

94 birth, born

95 bit, a little bit

96 birthday (CC)

97 bite

98 bitter, sour

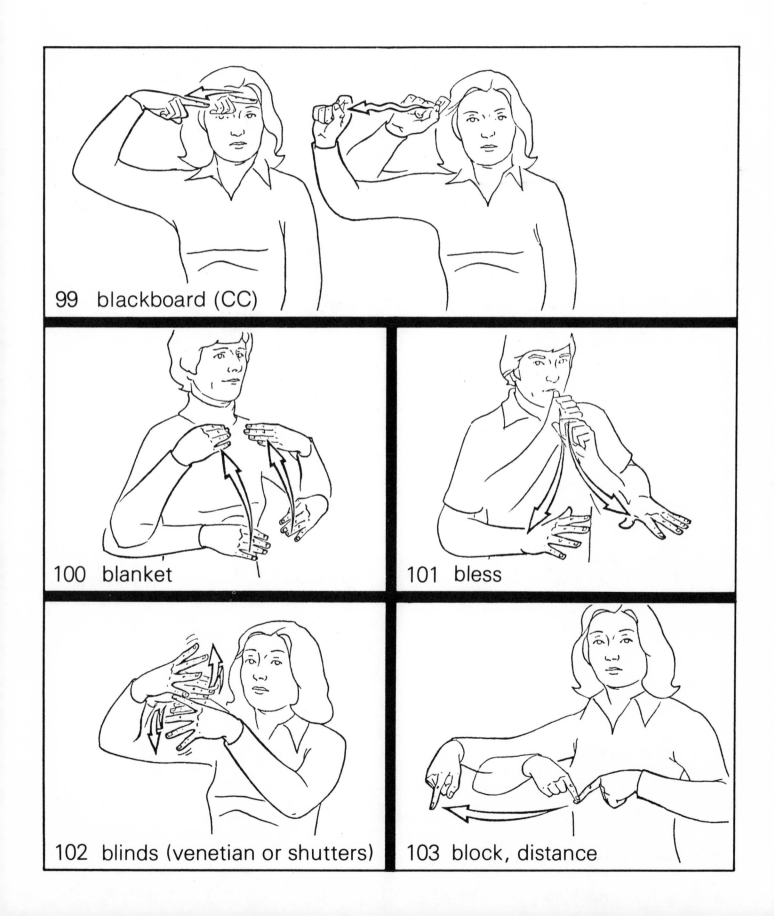

99 blackboard (CC)

100 blanket

101 bless

102 blinds (venetian or shutters)

103 block, distance

104 blocks (wood-) (CC)

105 blood, bleed

106 blue

107 board (wood) (CC)

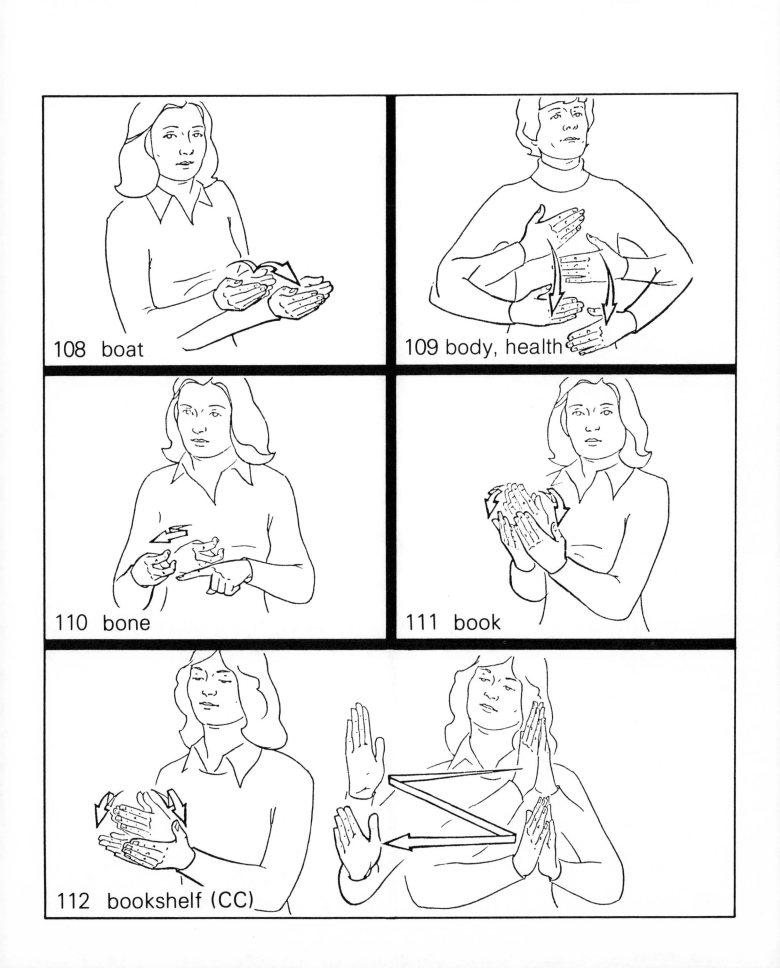

108 boat

109 body, health

110 bone

111 book

112 bookshelf (CC)

113 boots (CC)

114 borrow

115 boss, chief, general

116 bounce

117 bounce, dribble

118 both, pair

119 bottle

120 bottom

121 bowl

122 bow and arrow

123 bow, ribbon

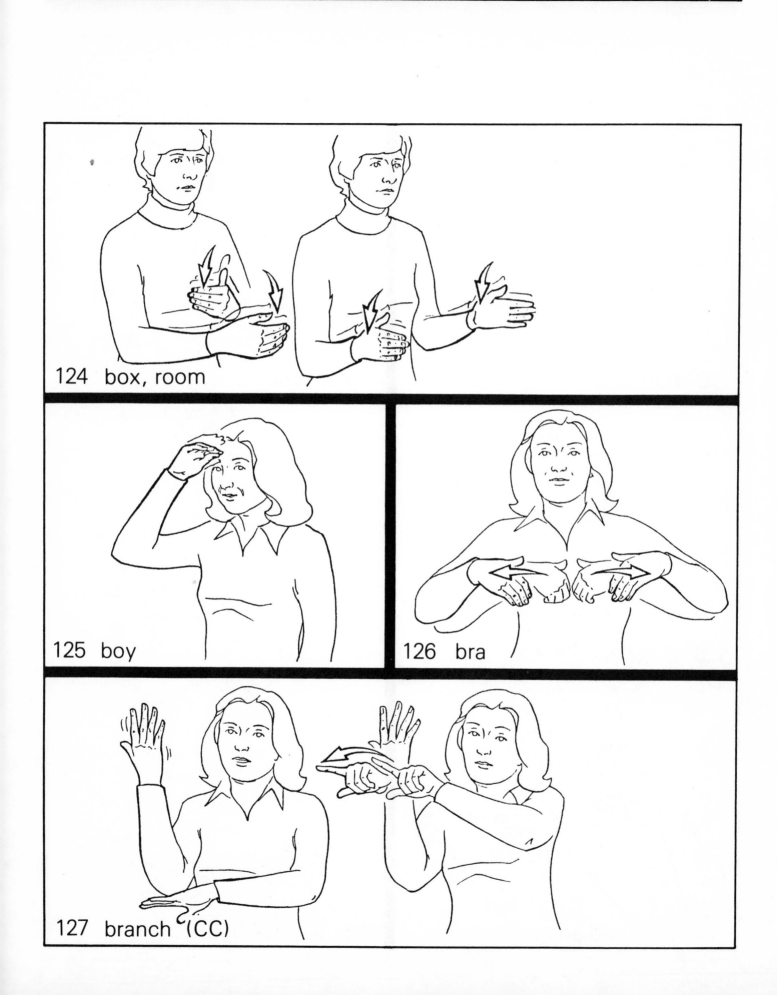

124 box, room

125 boy

126 bra

127 branch (CC)

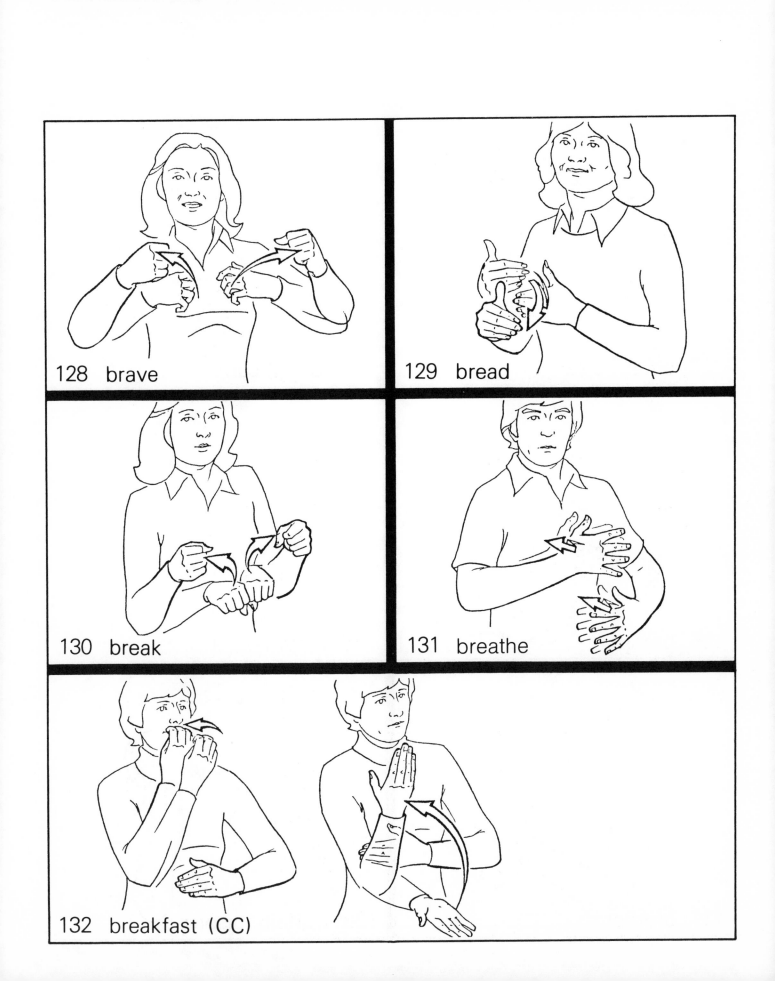

128 brave

129 bread

130 break

131 breathe

132 breakfast (CC)

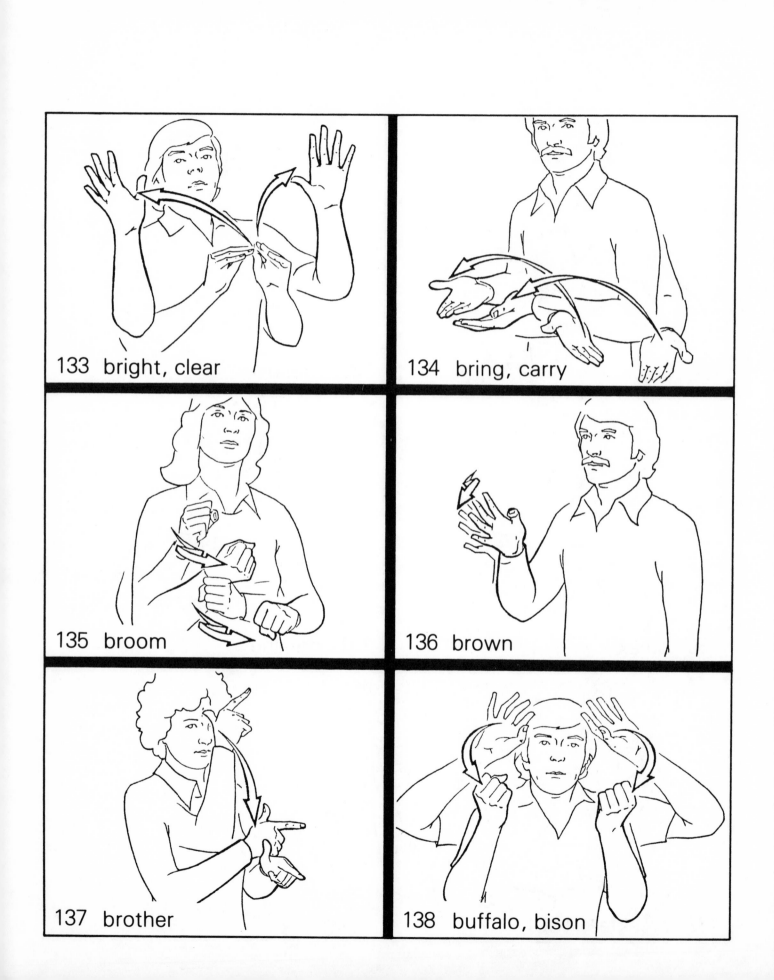

133 bright, clear

134 bring, carry

135 broom

136 brown

137 brother

138 buffalo, bison

139 bug

140 build, building (AM)

141 bus, truck (AM)

142 busy

143 butter

144 butterfly

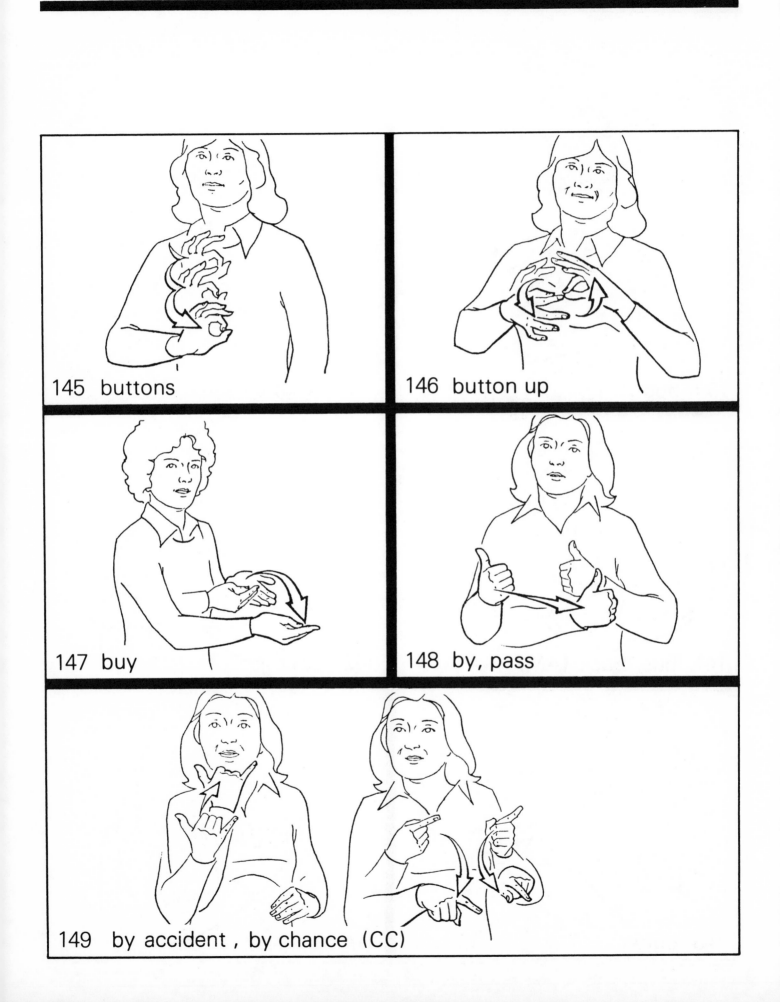

145 buttons

146 button up

147 buy

148 by, pass

149 by accident , by chance (CC)

Cc

150 cabbage, lettuce

151 cage

152 cake

153 camel

154 calendar (CC)

155 call, summon

call, telephone (V),
156 telephone (N) (DM)

157 call, yell

158 camera

159 can, able, possible (DM)

160 candle

161 candy

162 can't, cannot, impossible (DM)

163 cap

164 car (AM)

165 careful

166 carnival, circus, ferris wheel (AM)

167 carpenter

168 carrot

169 cat

170 caterpillar

171 catch

172 cause

173 center, central

174 cereal

175 chain (AM)

176 change

177 chase

178 chat

179 cheese

180 cherry

181 chicken

182 chief (most important)

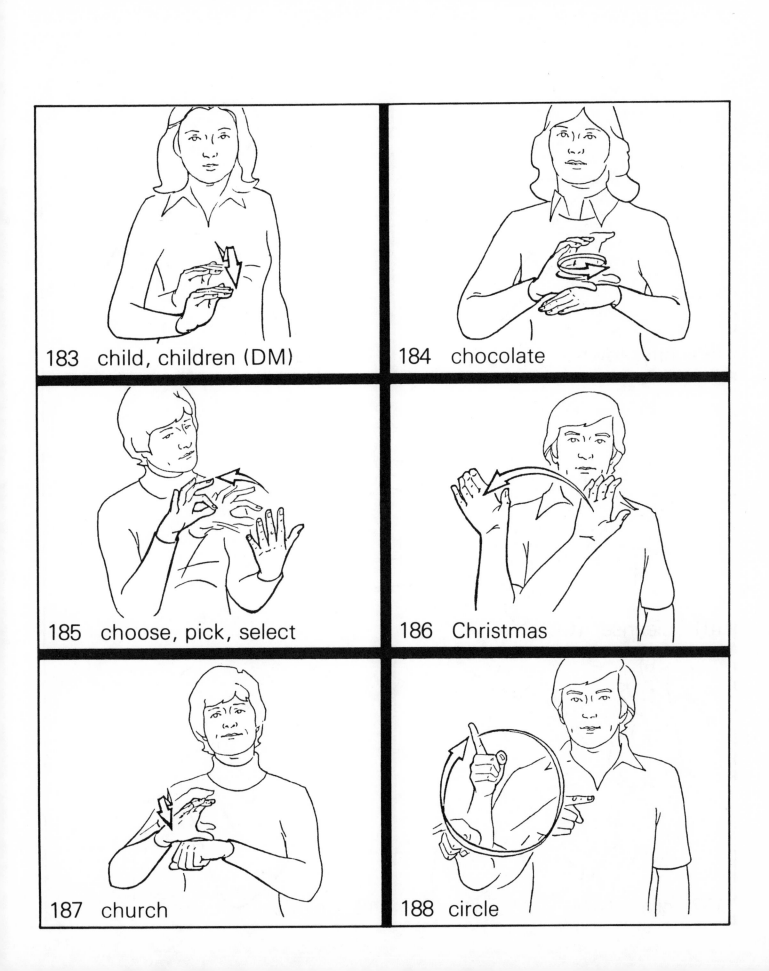

183 child, children (DM)

184 chocolate

185 choose, pick, select

186 Christmas

187 church

188 circle

189 city, town

190 class, group

191 cleanser (CC)

192 climb (AM)

193 cloth

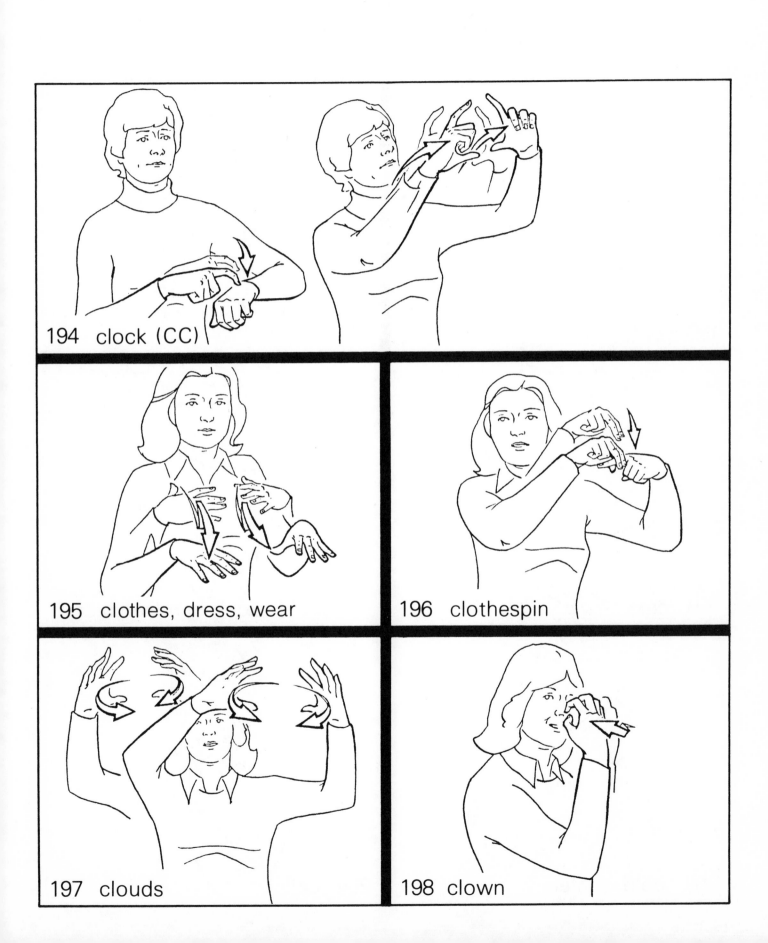

194 clock (CC)

195 clothes, dress, wear

196 clothespin

197 clouds

198 clown

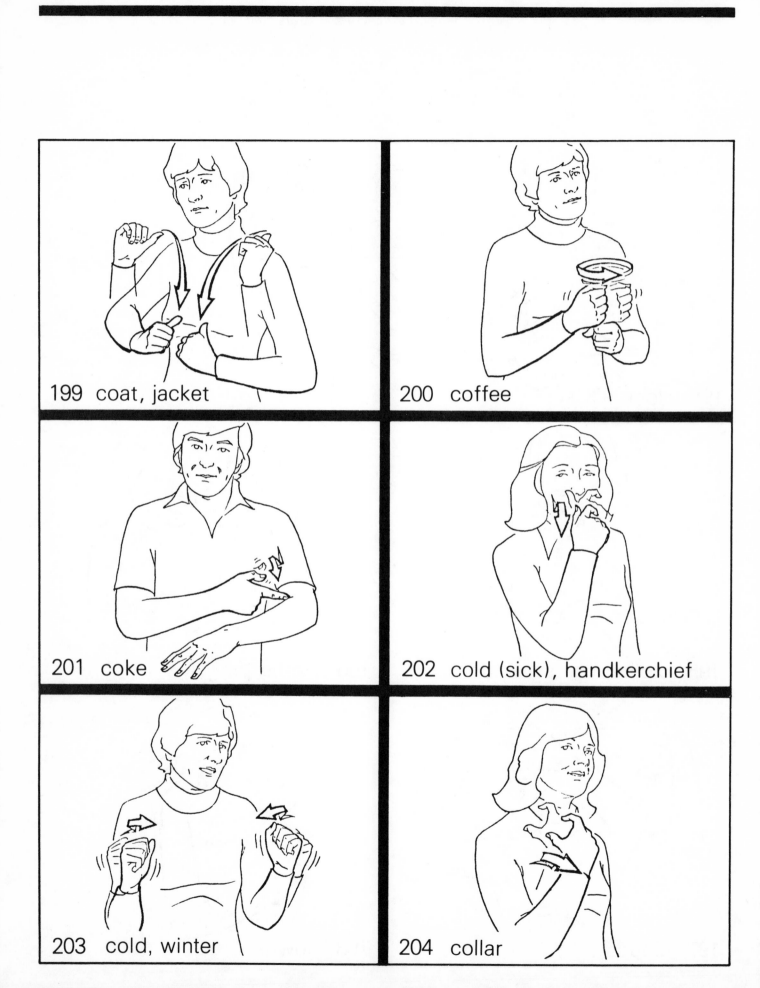

199 coat, jacket

200 coffee

201 coke

202 cold (sick), handkerchief

203 cold, winter

204 collar

205 color

206 comb (V)

207 come

208 commend, praise, applaud

209 common, standard (all the same).

210 complain, gripe

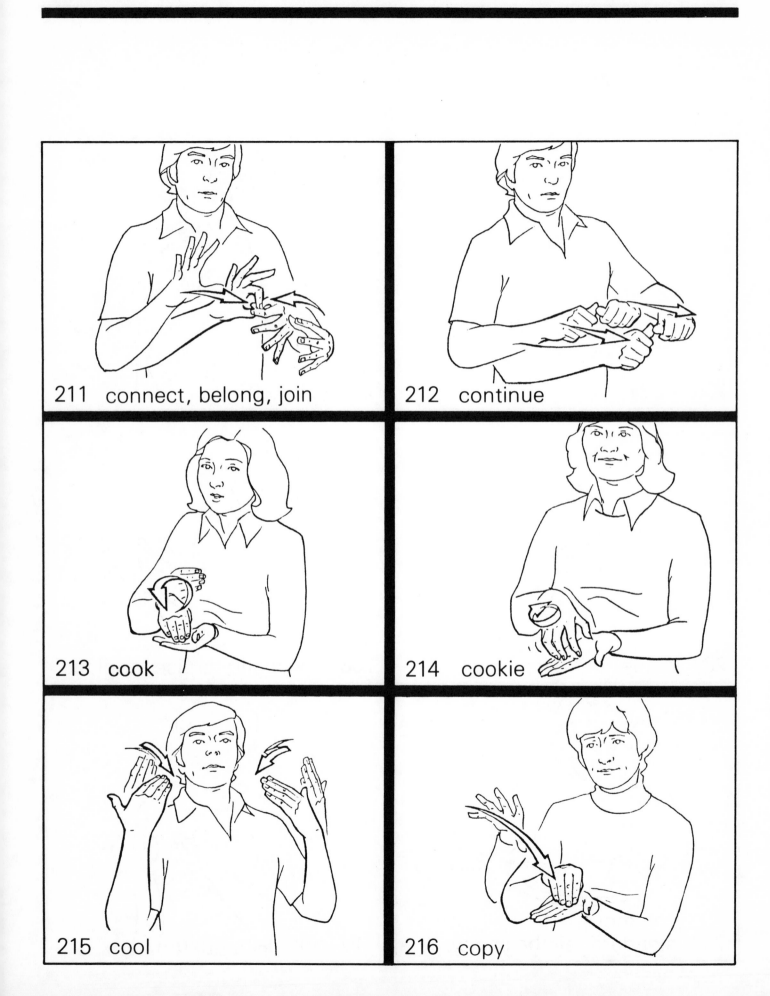

211 connect, belong, join

212 continue

213 cook

214 cookie

215 cool

216 copy

217 corn

218 corner

219 cost, price, charge

220 cotton

221 cough

222 count

223 country

224 cousin

225 cover, cover up

226 cow

227 cowboy (CC)

228 crab

229 crackers

230 crayon (CC)

231 cream

232 crown

233 cry, tears (AM)

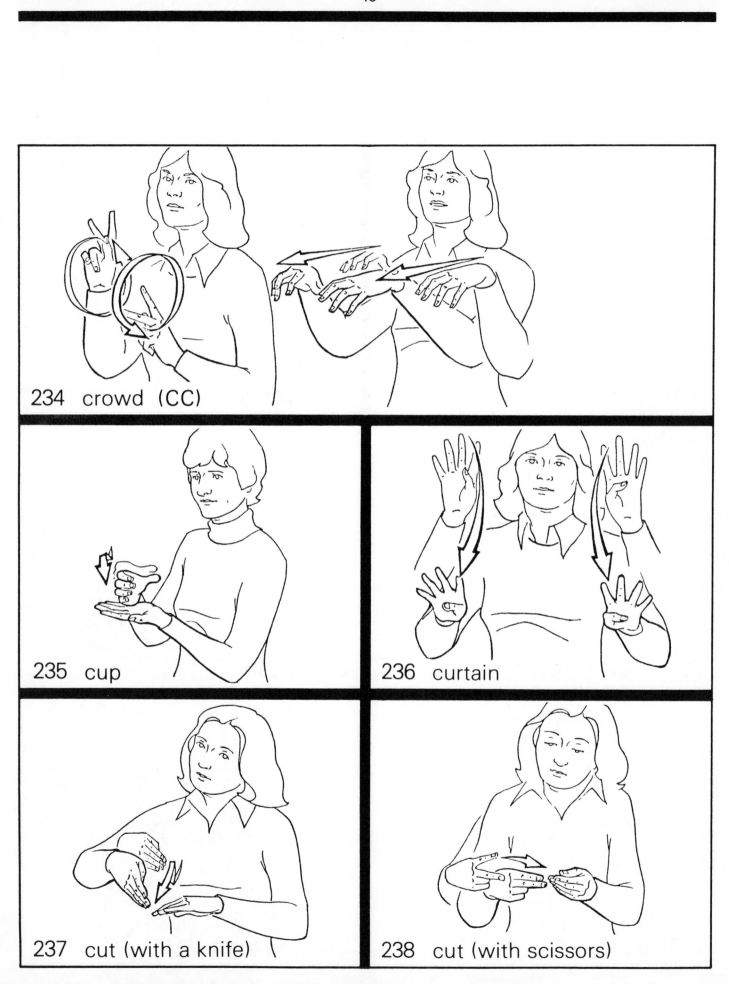

234 crowd (CC)

235 cup

236 curtain

237 cut (with a knife)

238 cut (with scissors)

Dd

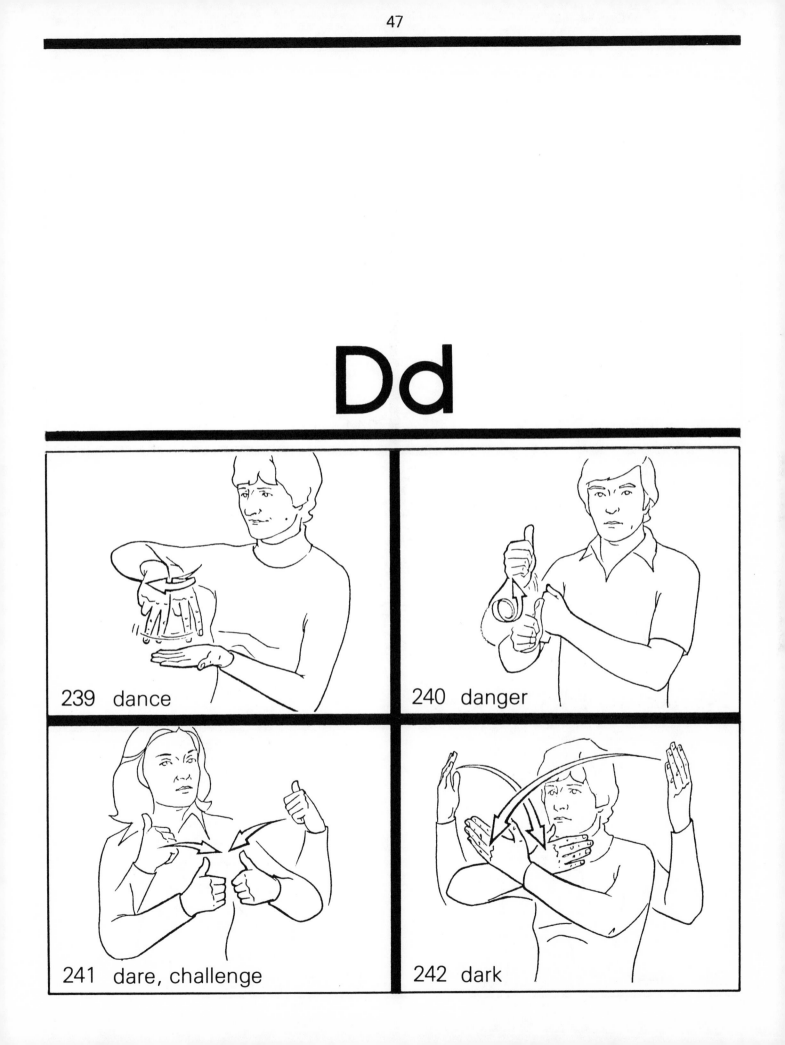

239 dance

240 danger

241 dare, challenge

242 dark

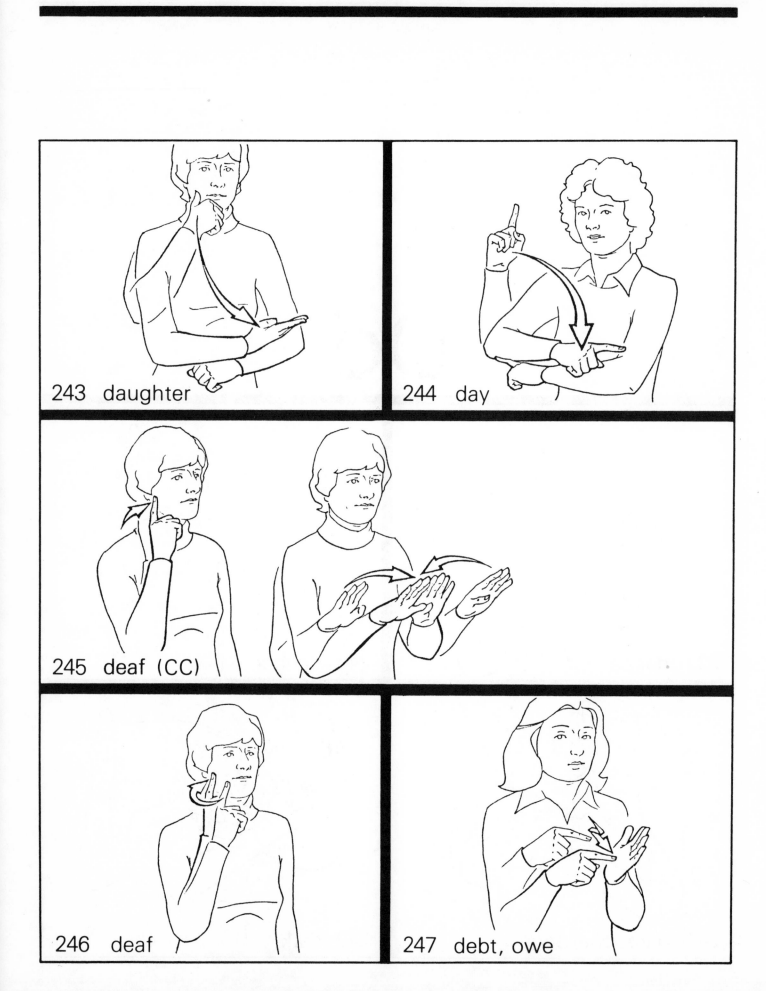

243 daughter

244 day

245 deaf (CC)

246 deaf

247 debt, owe

248 dead, death

249 decide, decision (CC)

250 deer

251 demand, require

252 dentist

253 destroy

254 desert (CC)

255 dictionary

256 different

257 dive

258 dirty, filthy, soiled

259 dinner, supper (CC)

260 direct, control (AM)

261 direct, straight-to

262 disappoint, miss

263 divide, share (DM)

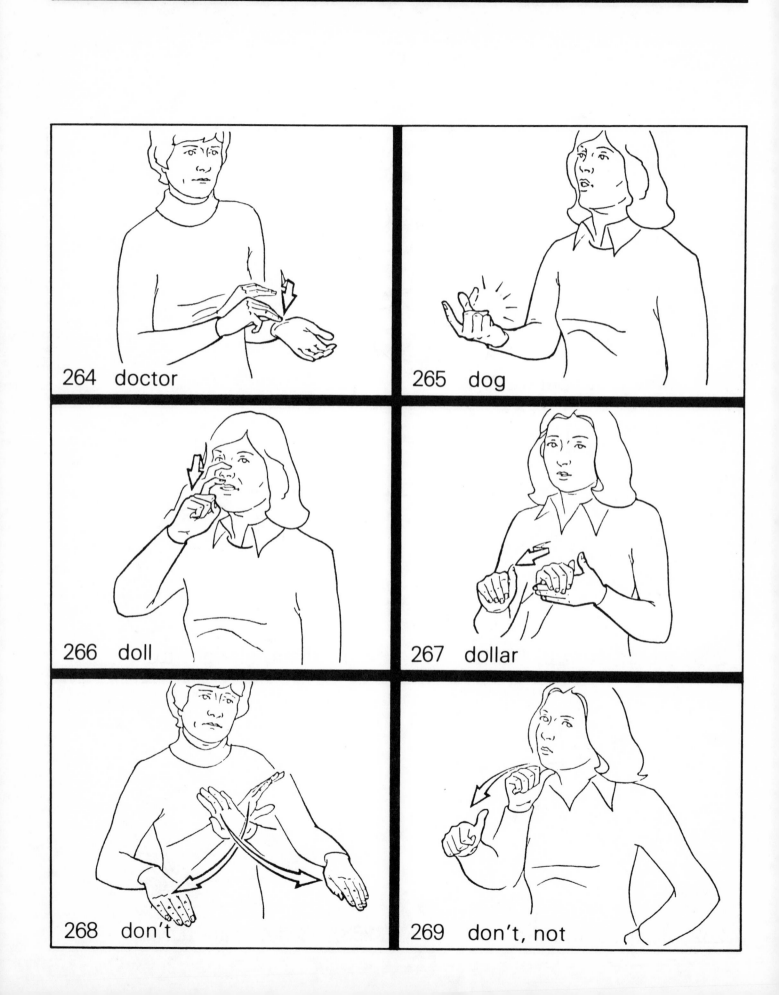

264 doctor

265 dog

266 doll

267 dollar

268 don't

269 don't, not

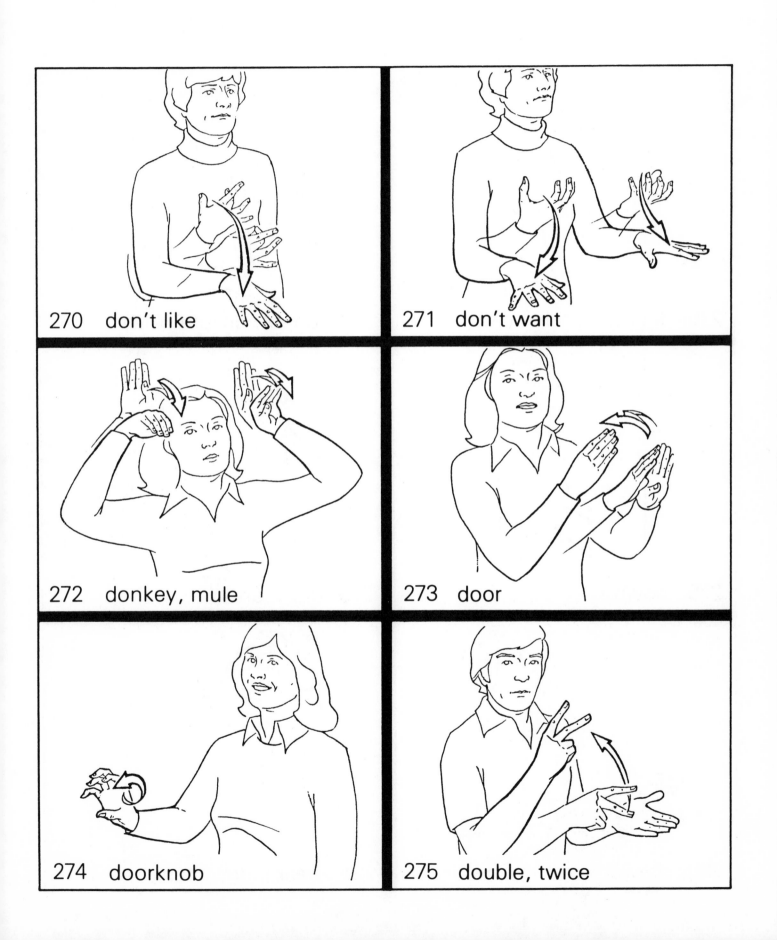

270   don't like

271   don't want

272   donkey, mule

273   door

274   doorknob

275   double, twice

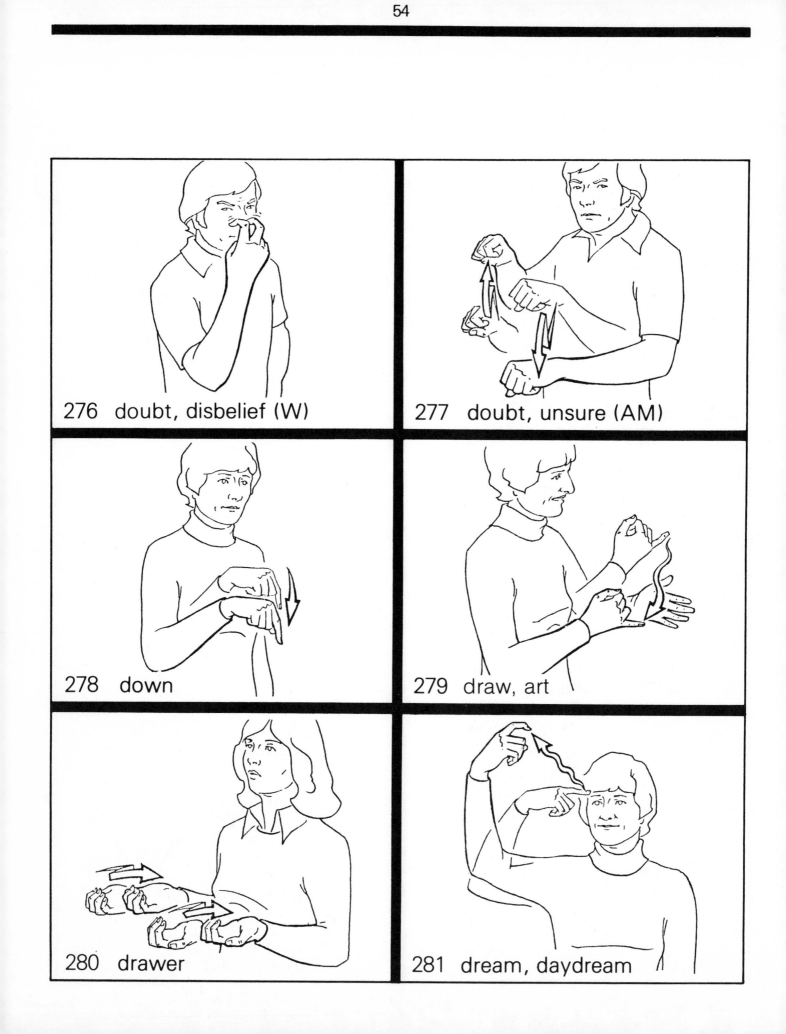

276 doubt, disbelief (W)

277 doubt, unsure (AM)

278 down

279 draw, art

280 drawer

281 dream, daydream

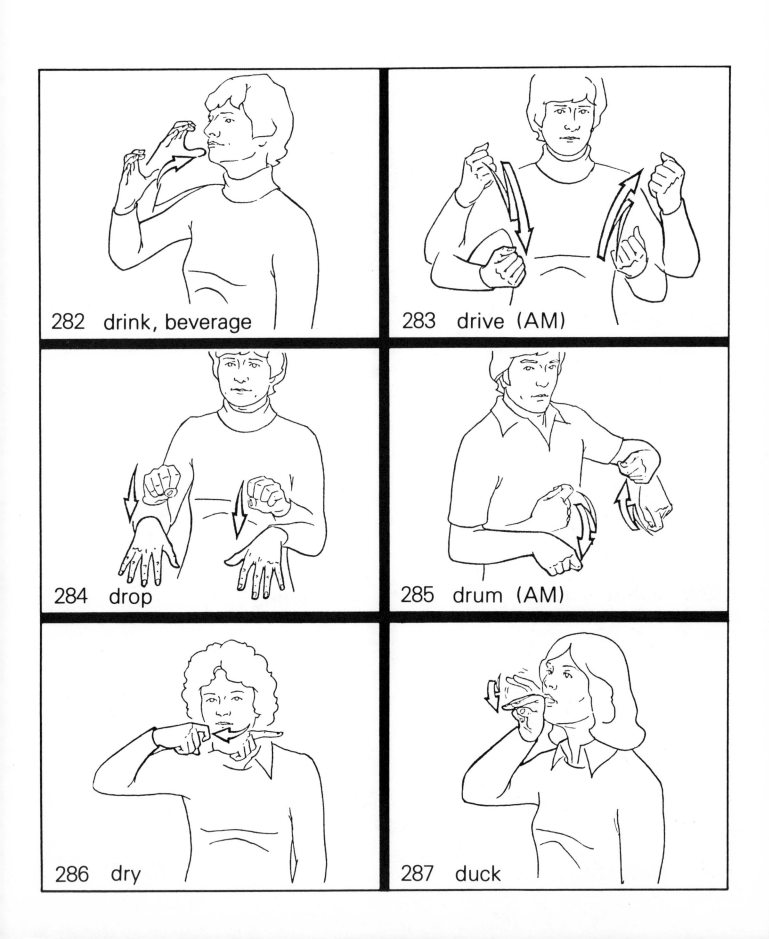

282 drink, beverage

283 drive (AM)

284 drop

285 drum (AM)

286 dry

287 duck

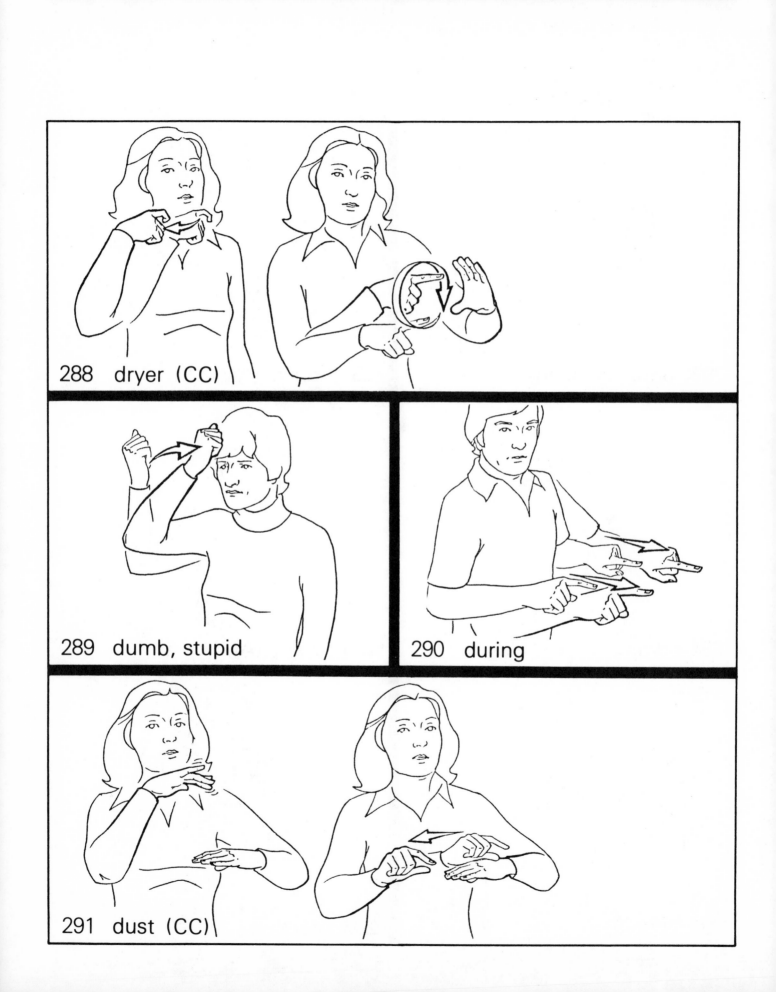

288 dryer (CC)

289 dumb, stupid

290 during

291 dust (CC)

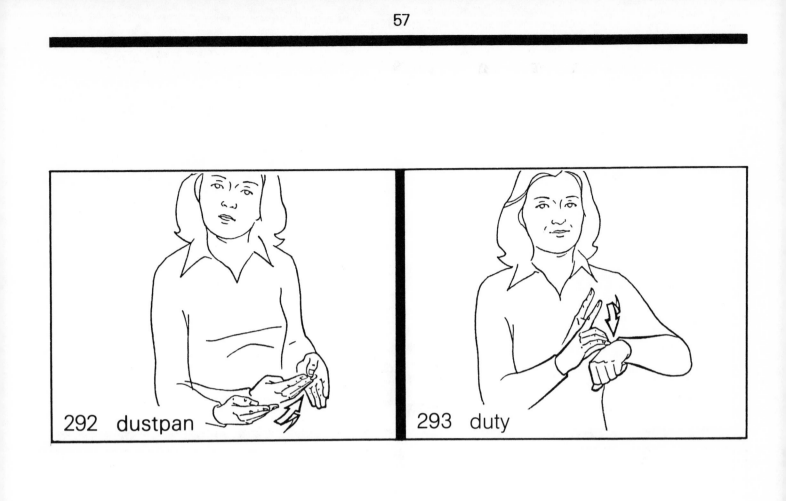

292 dustpan

293 duty

Ee

294   each, every

295   eager, enthusiasm

296   eagle

297   ear

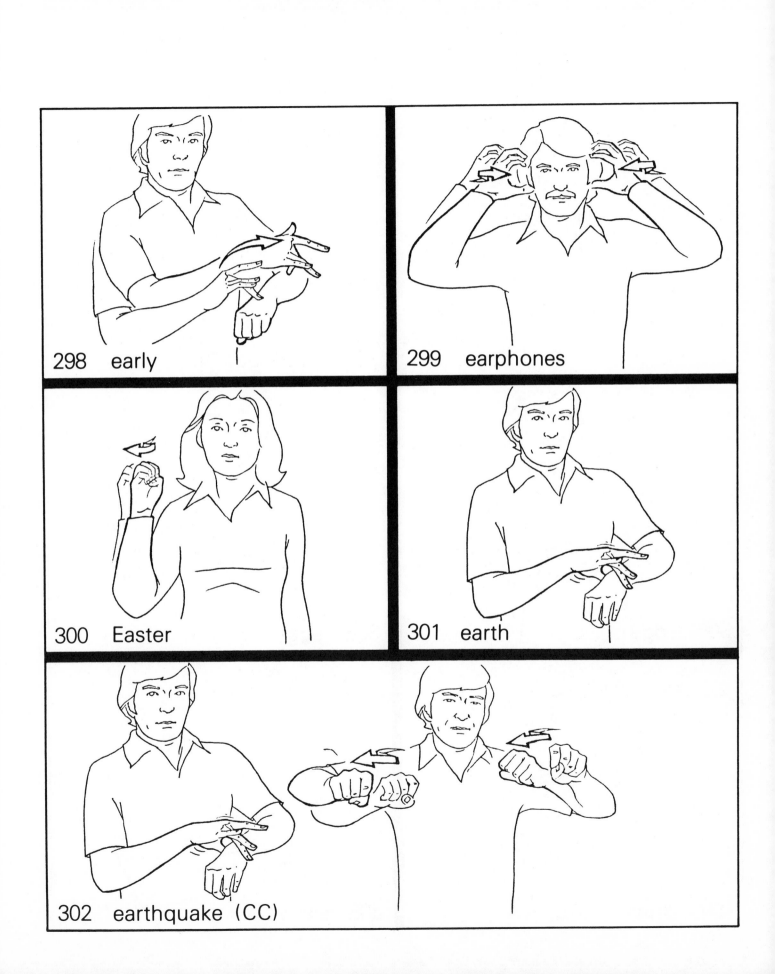

298 early

299 earphones

300 Easter

301 earth

302 earthquake (CC)

303 East

304 eat, food (DM)

305 edge

306 egg

307 either

308 elbow

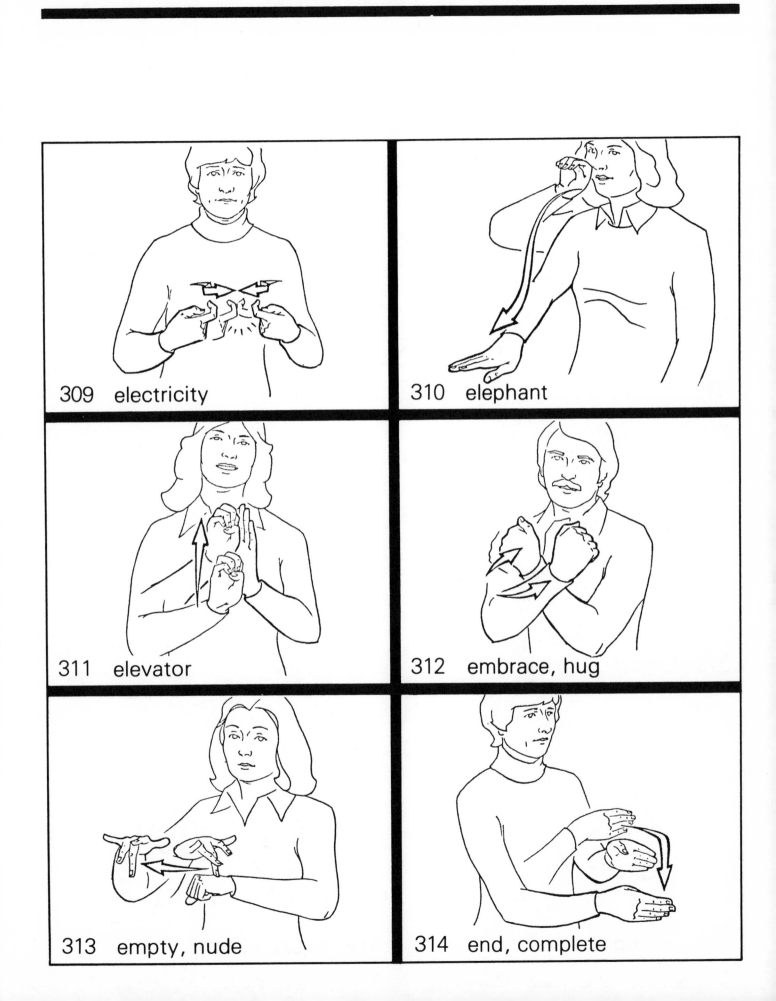

309 electricity

310 elephant

311 elevator

312 embrace, hug

313 empty, nude

314 end, complete

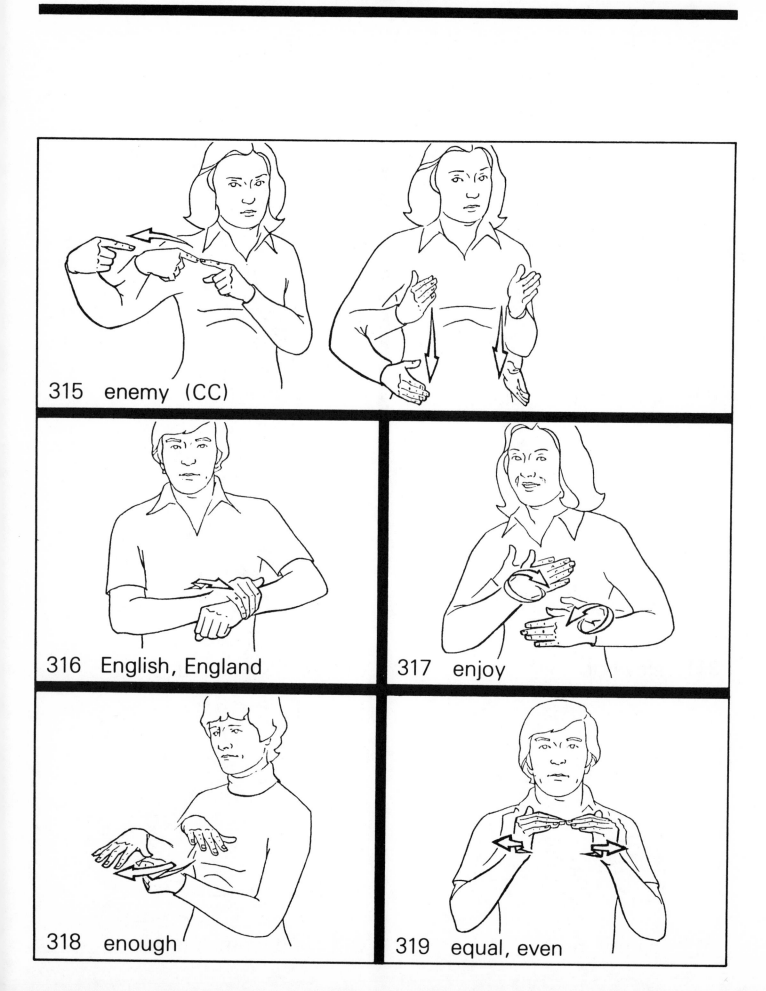

315 enemy (CC)

316 English, England

317 enjoy

318 enough

319 equal, even

320   envelope (CC)

321   eraser

322   escalator

323   escape

324   everyday

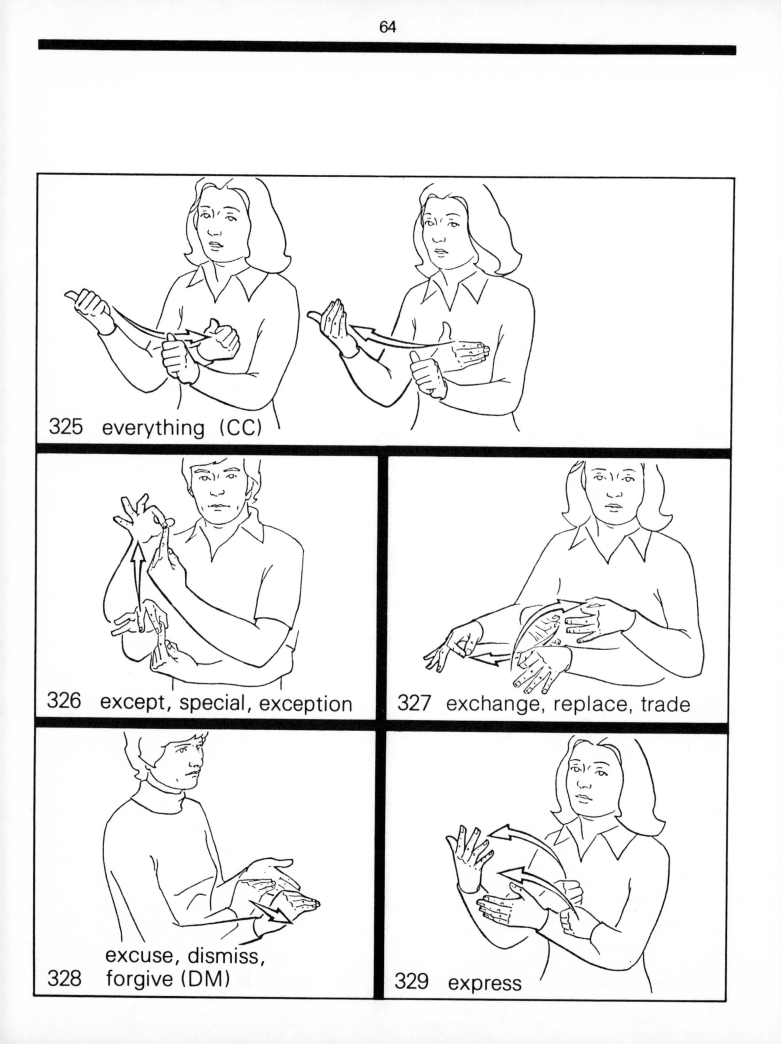

325 everything (CC)

326 except, special, exception

327 exchange, replace, trade

328 excuse, dismiss, forgive (DM)

329 express

330   eyes

331   extend

Ff

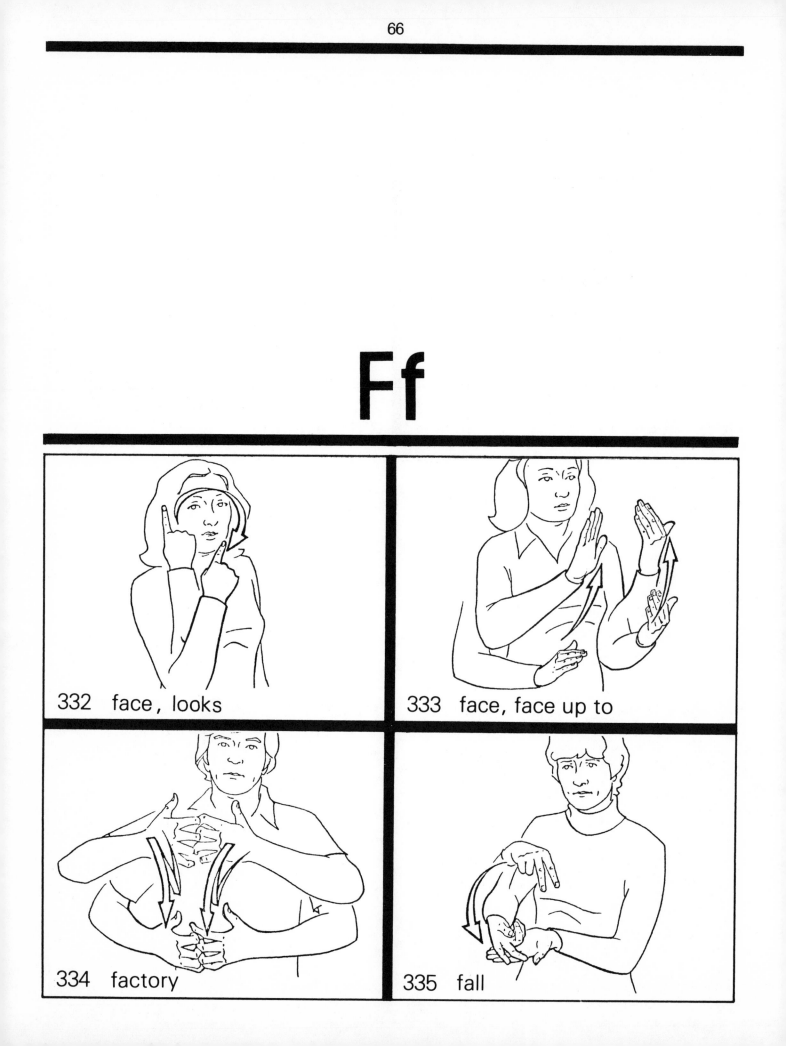

332 face, looks

333 face, face up to

334 factory

335 fall

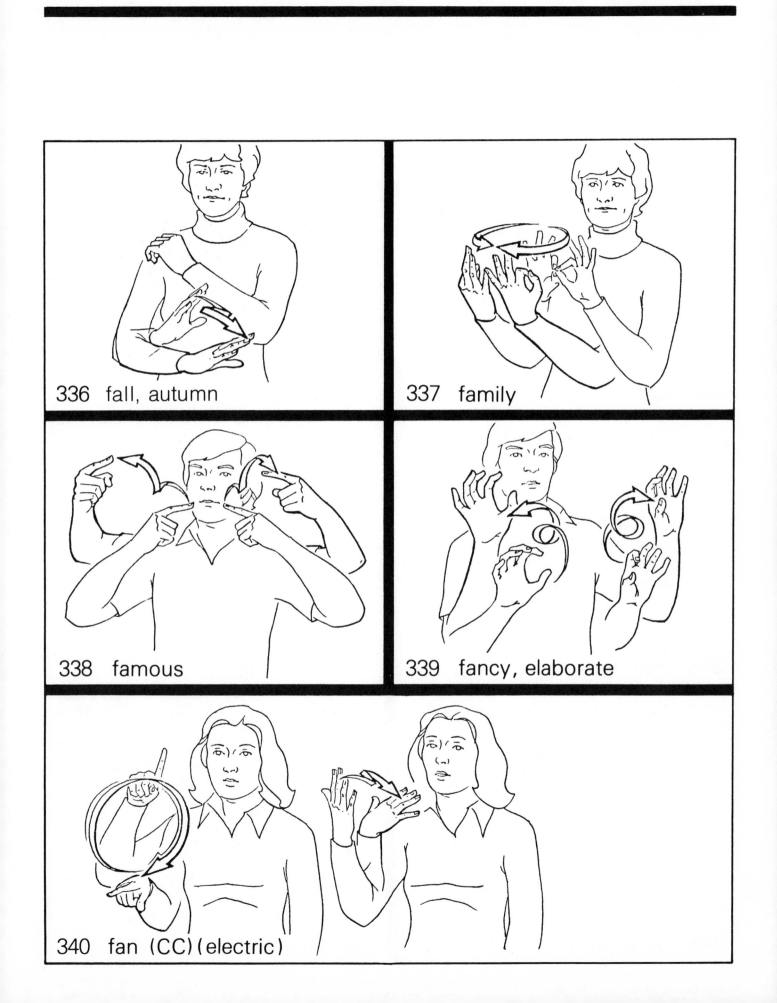

336 fall, autumn

337 family

338 famous

339 fancy, elaborate

340 fan (CC)(electric)

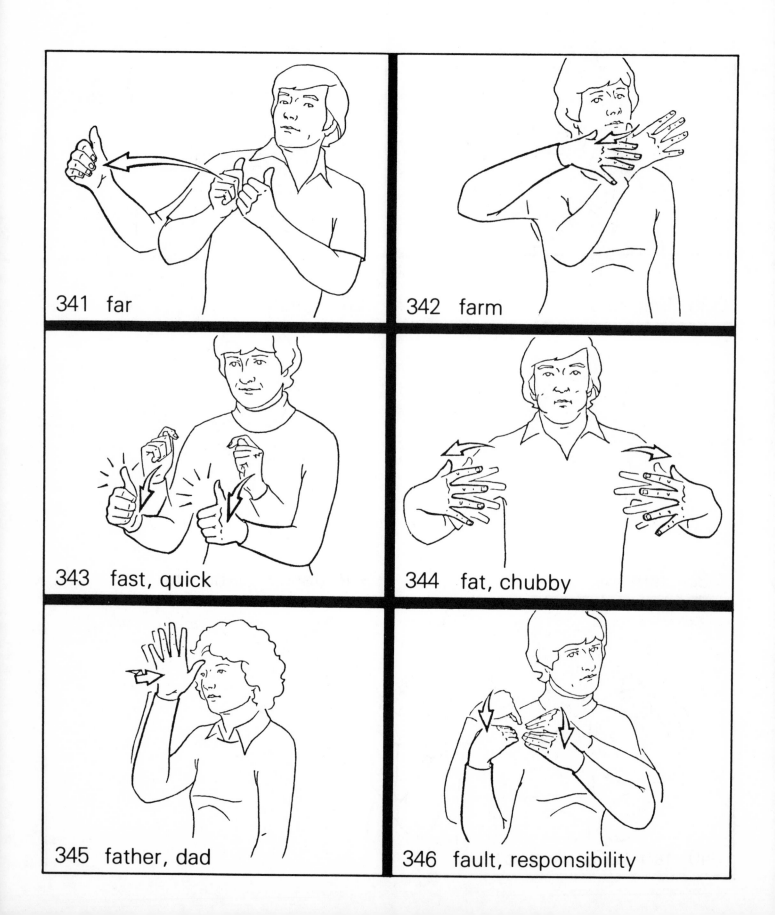

341 far

342 farm

343 fast, quick

344 fat, chubby

345 father, dad

346 fault, responsibility

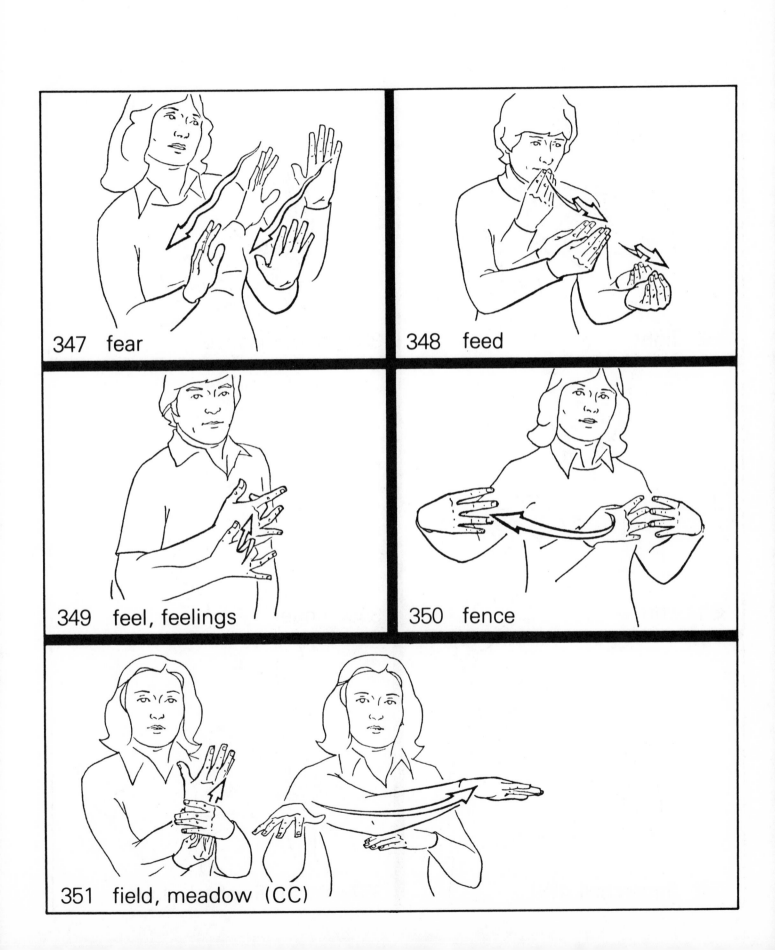

347 fear

348 feed

349 feel, feelings

350 fence

351 field, meadow (CC)

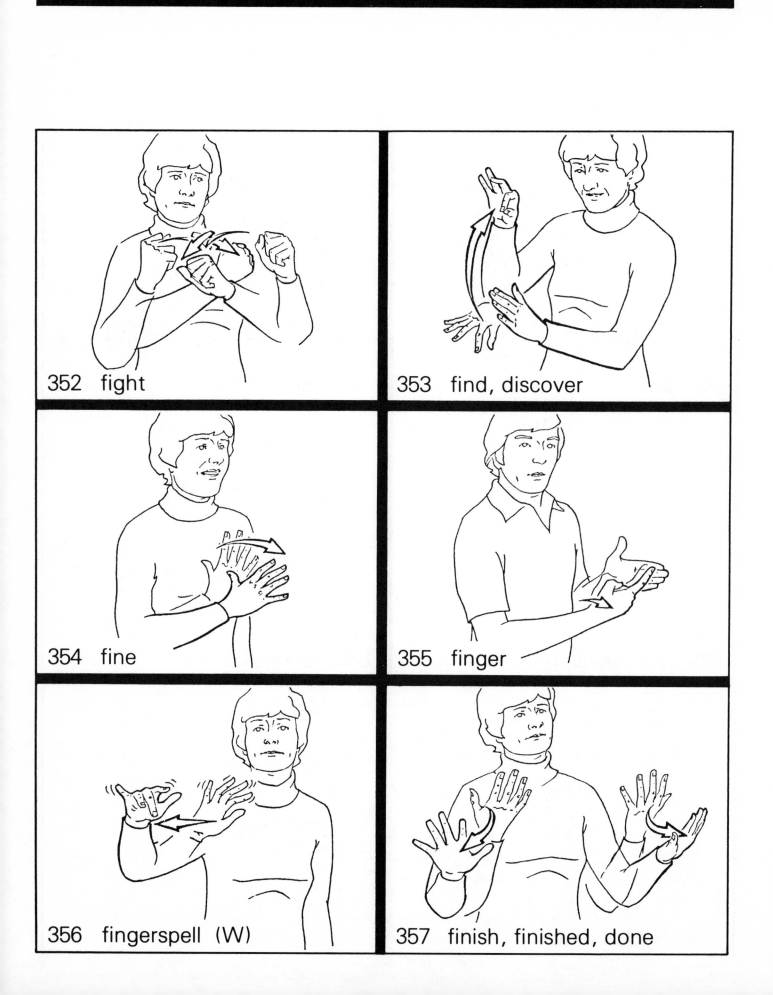

352 fight

353 find, discover

354 fine

355 finger

356 fingerspell (W)

357 finish, finished, done

358 fireplace (CC) (W)

359 fire (AM) (W)

360 firm, strict

361 fish

362 fit , exact, perfect

363 flag

364 flashlight

365 flat

366 float

367 floor

368 flower

369   fly (by plane)

370   follow

371   foot

372   football

373   for

374   forest

375 forever (CC)

376 force

377 forget

378 fork

379 fox

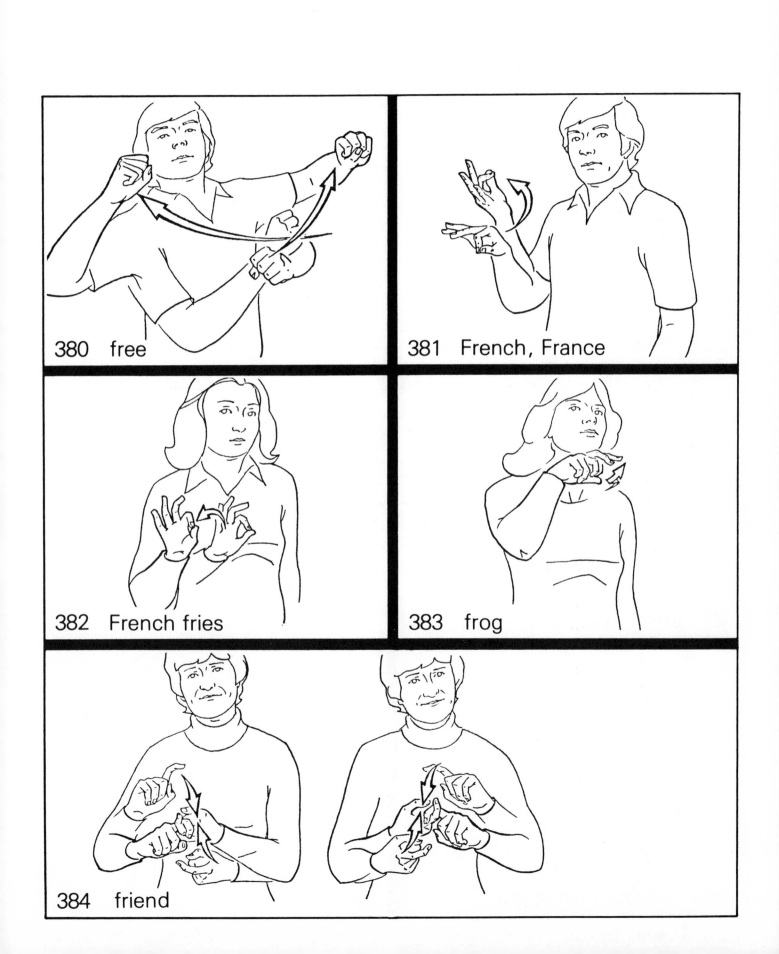

380 free

381 French, France

382 French fries

383 frog

384 friend

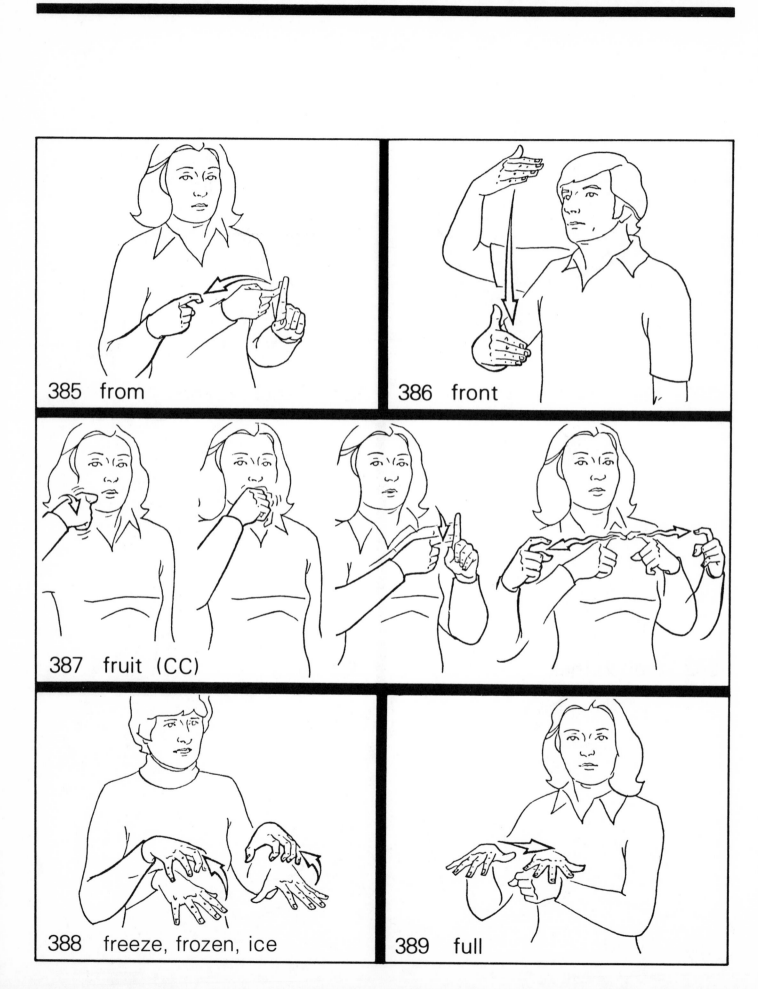

385 from

386 front

387 fruit (CC)

388 freeze, frozen, ice

389 full

390 fun

391 funny

392 furniture

Gg

393 gain, increase

394 game

395 garden (flower-)(CC)

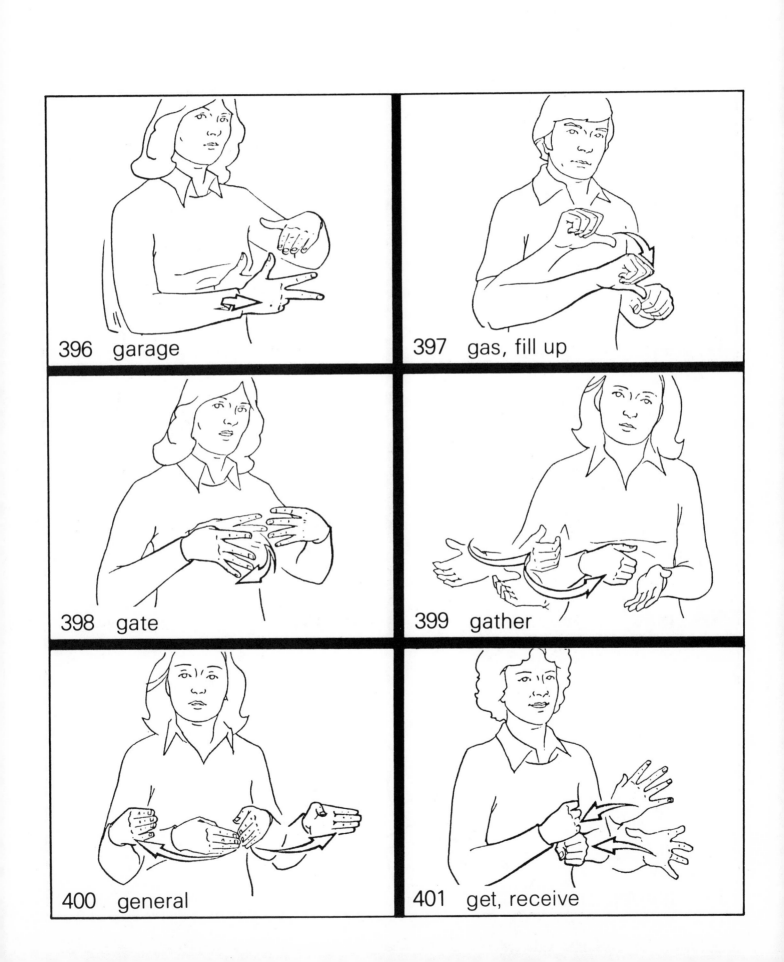

396 garage

397 gas, fill up

398 gate

399 gather

400 general

401 get, receive

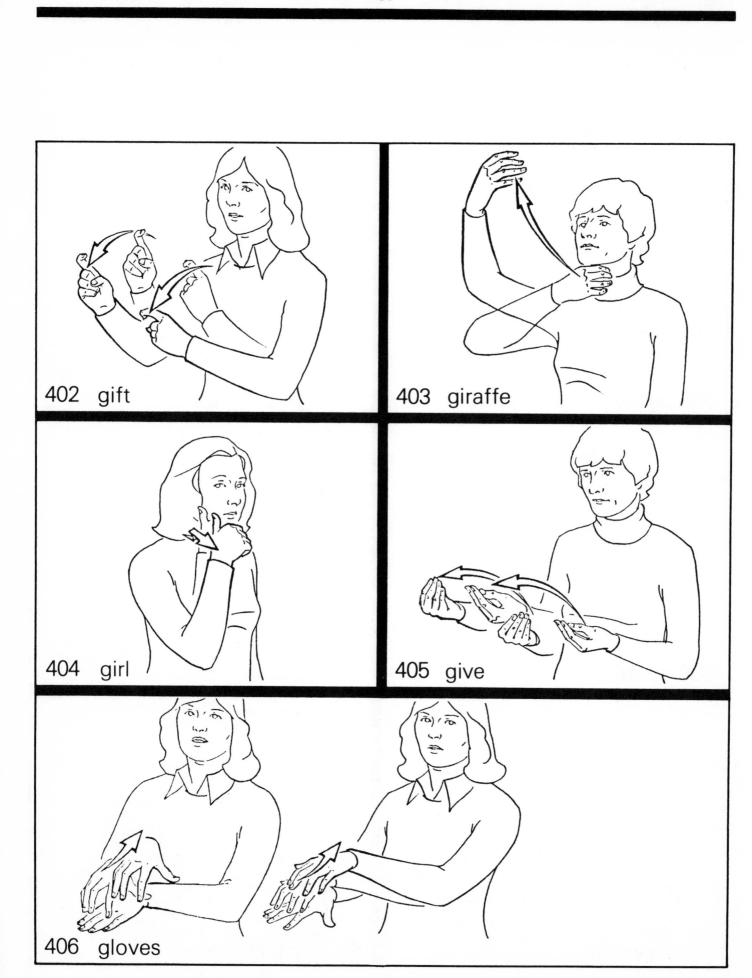

402 gift

403 giraffe

404 girl

405 give

406 gloves

407   glasses

408   goat

409   glue (CC)

410   go

411   go (AM)

412 God

413 gold, California

414 good

415 goodbye, bye-bye

416 goose, swan

417 grab

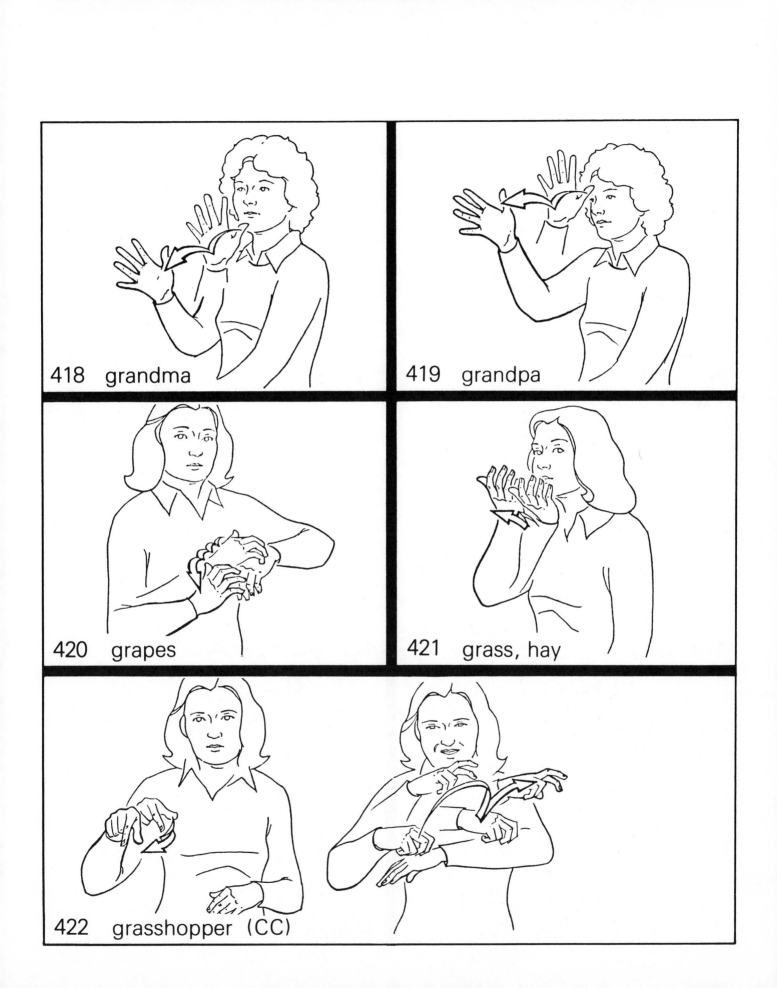

418 grandma

419 grandpa

420 grapes

421 grass, hay

422 grasshopper (CC)

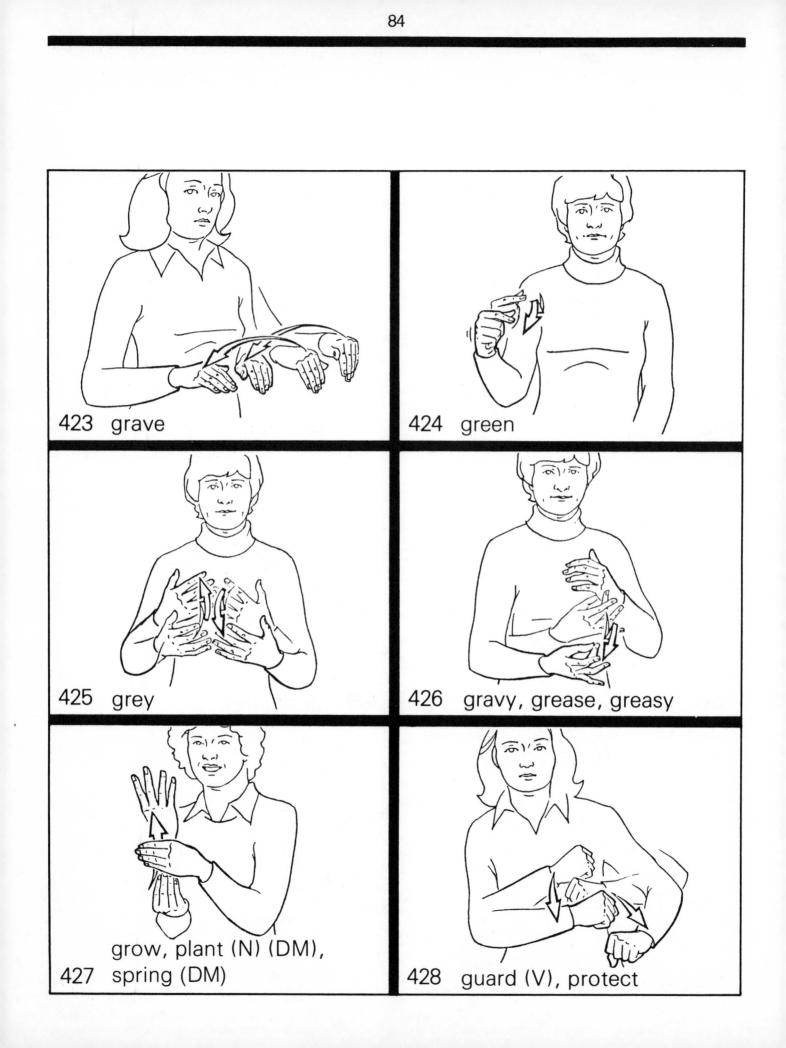

423 grave

424 green

425 grey

426 gravy, grease, greasy

427 grow, plant (N) (DM), spring (DM)

428 guard (V), protect

429   guess

430   guide, lead

431   gum

Hh

432 hair

433 hairbrush, comb (N)

434 half

435 hall

436 hamburger

437 hammer

438 hamster (CC)

439 hands

440 hang up, hanger (DM)

441 happen

442 happy, glad, joy

443 hard, firm

444 hard-of-hearing

445 hat

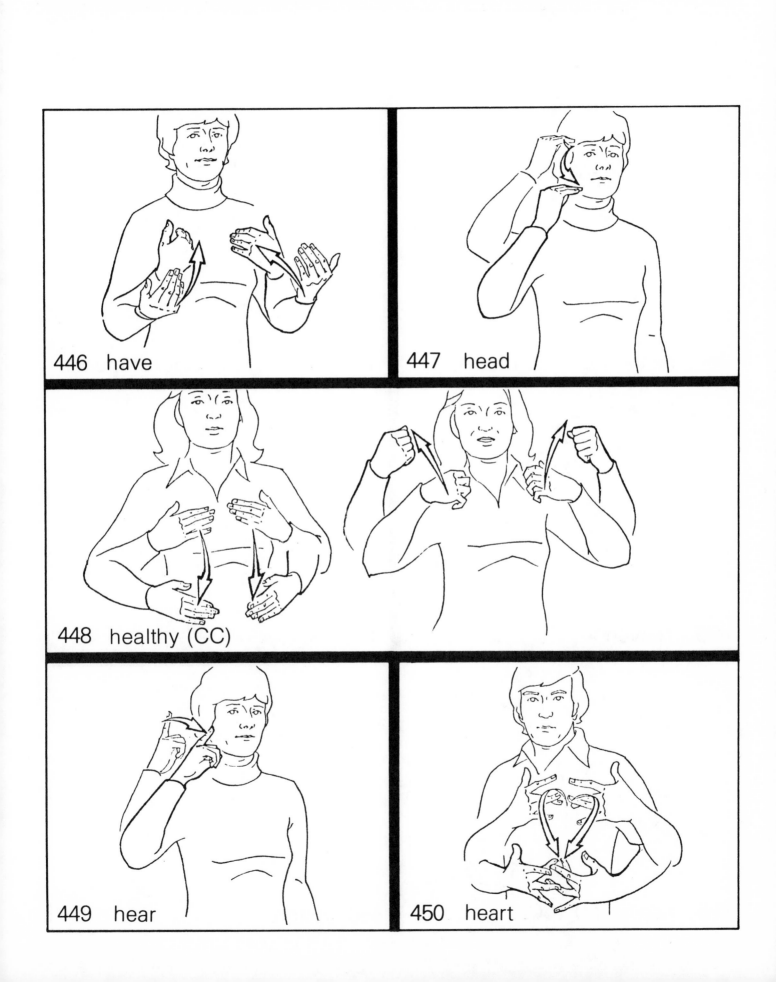

446 have

447 head

448 healthy (CC)

449 hear

450 heart

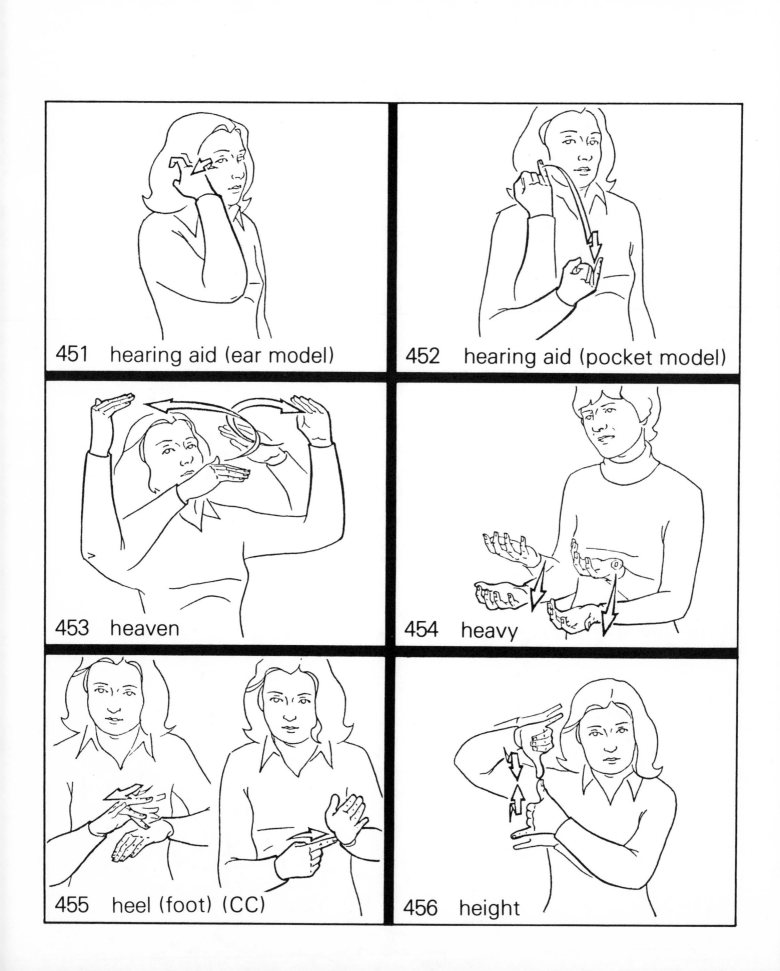

451 hearing aid (ear model)

452 hearing aid (pocket model)

453 heaven

454 heavy

455 heel (foot) (CC)

456 height

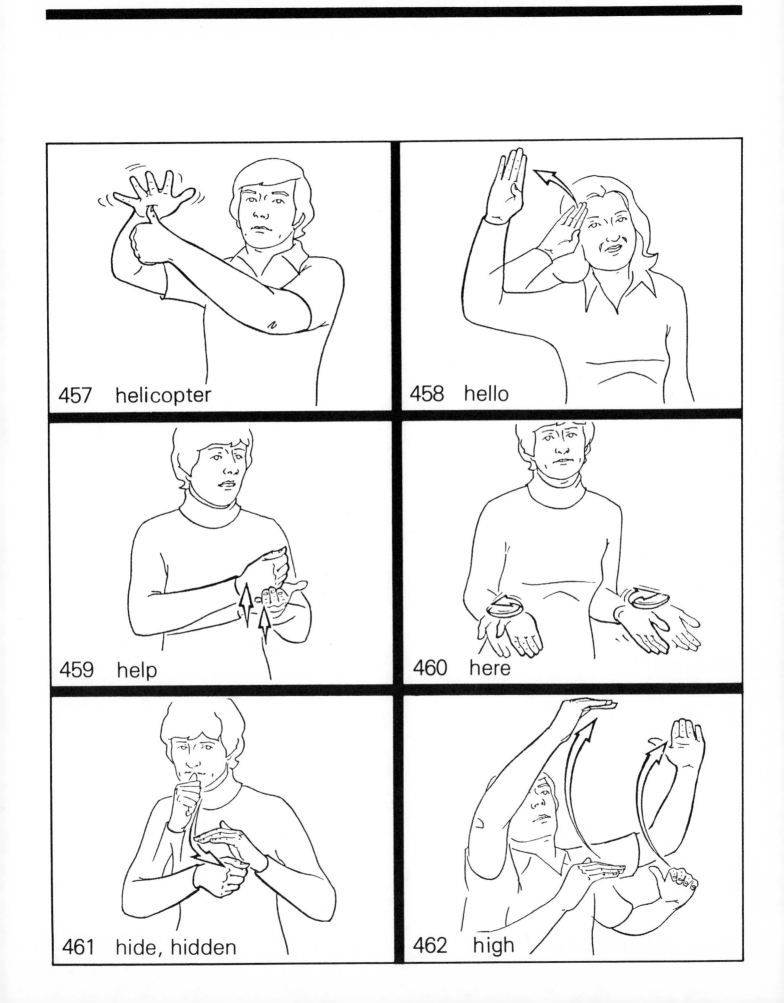

457 helicopter

458 hello

459 help

460 here

461 hide, hidden

462 high

463 hike (AM)(CC)

464 hill

465 hit

466 hippopotamus (CC)

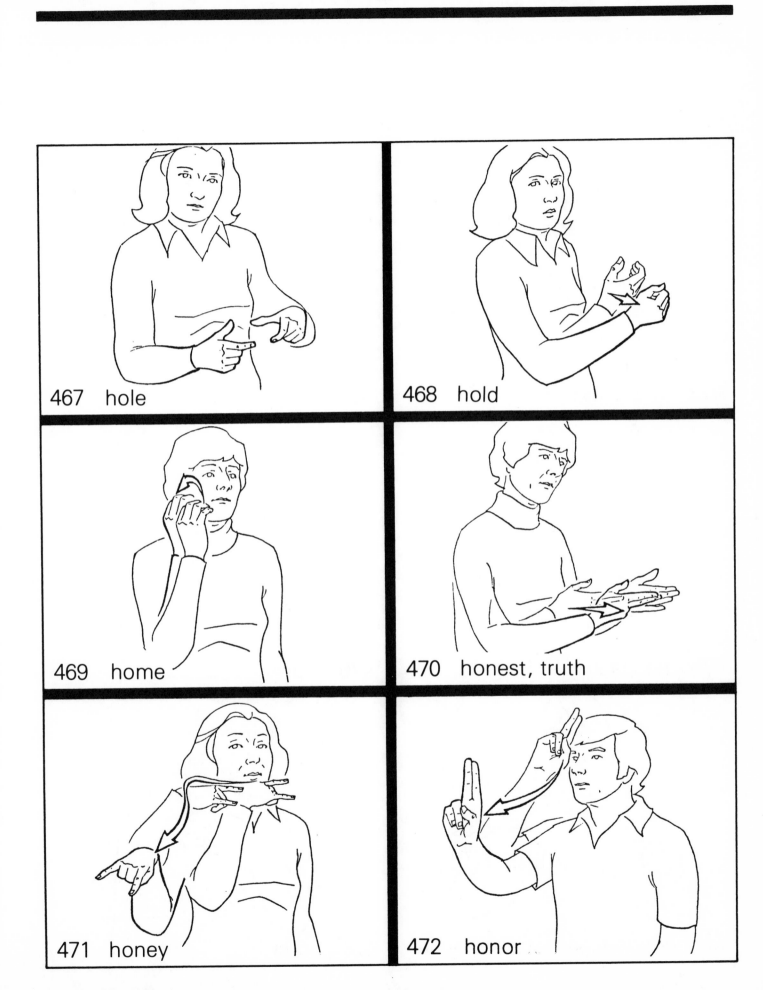

467   hole

468   hold

469   home

470   honest, truth

471   honey

472   honor

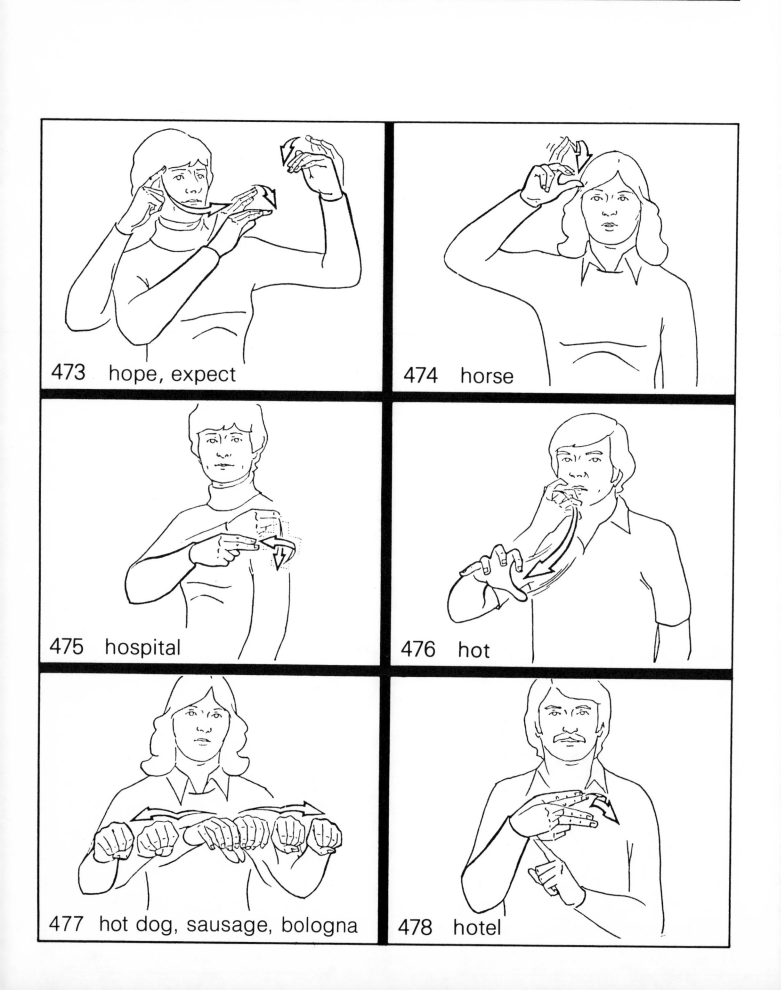

473 hope, expect

474 horse

475 hospital

476 hot

477 hot dog, sausage, bologna

478 hotel

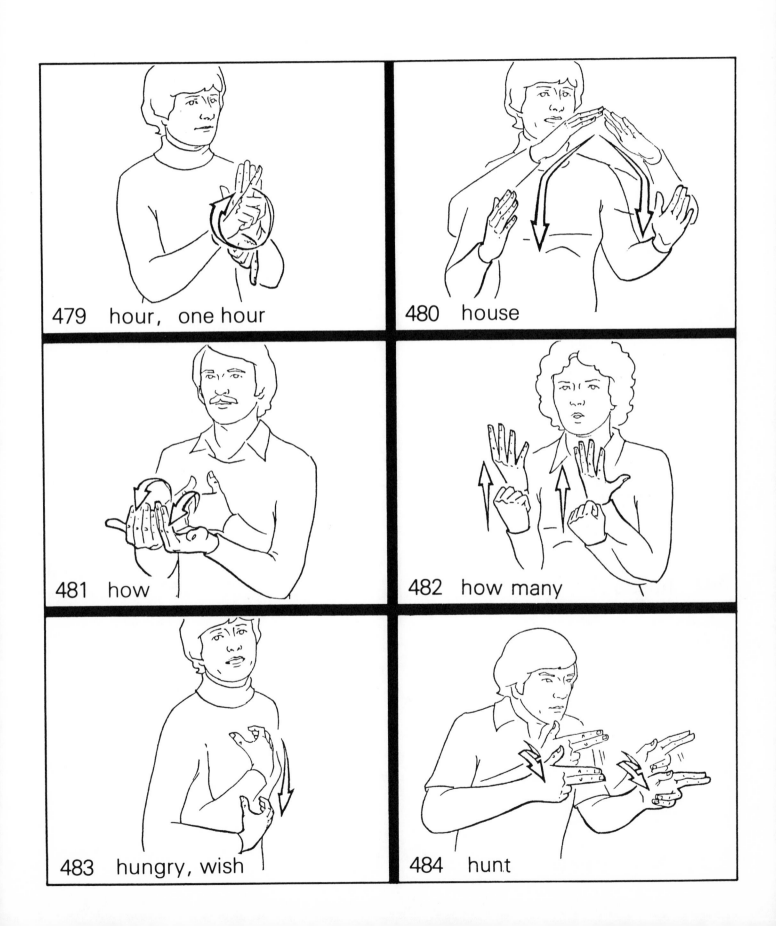

479 hour, one hour

480 house

481 how

482 how many

483 hungry, wish

484 hunt

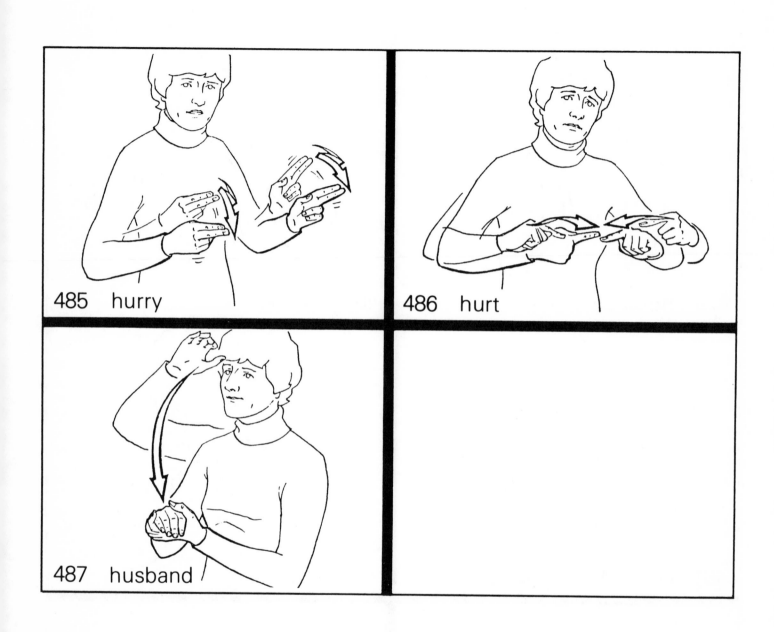

485   hurry

486   hurt

487   husband

Ii

488   I

489   ice cream

490   if

491   important, worth

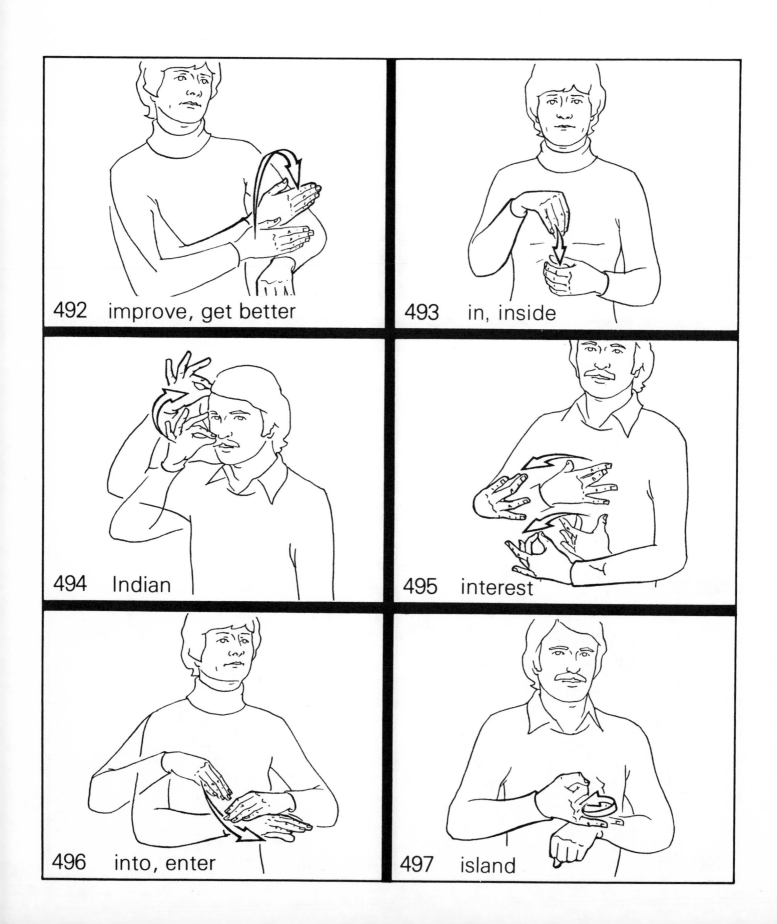

492 improve, get better

493 in, inside

494 Indian

495 interest

496 into, enter

497 island

498   invite

Jj

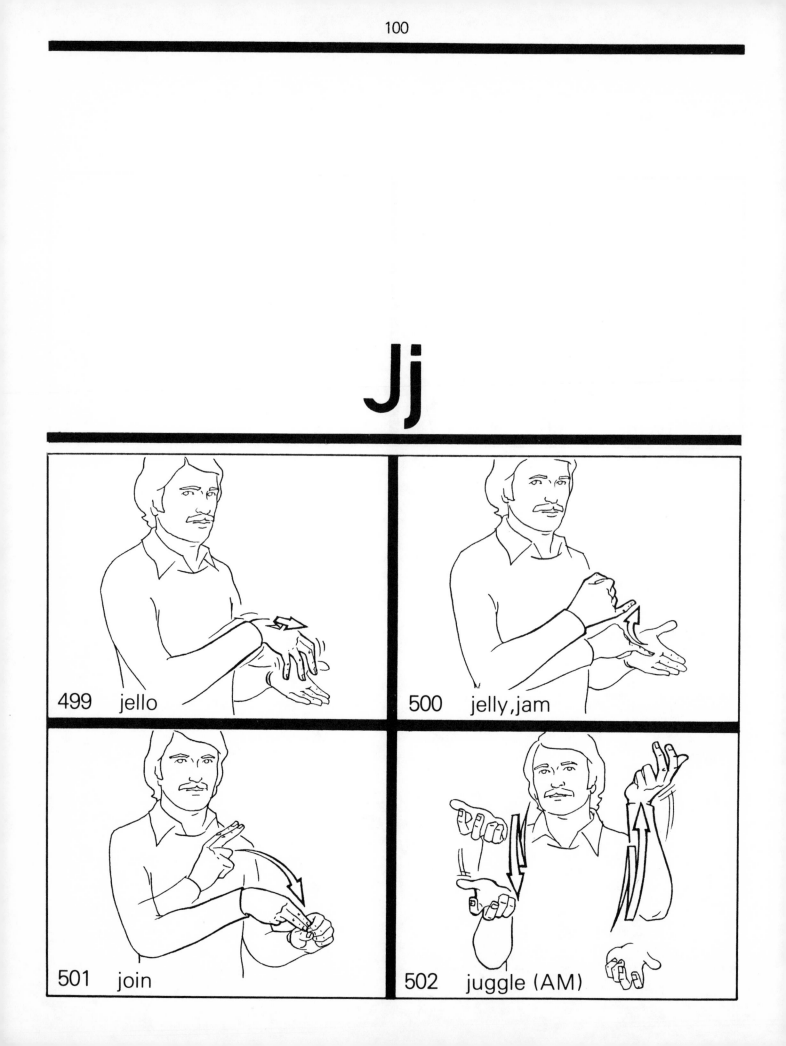

499　jello

500　jelly,jam

501　join

502　juggle (AM)

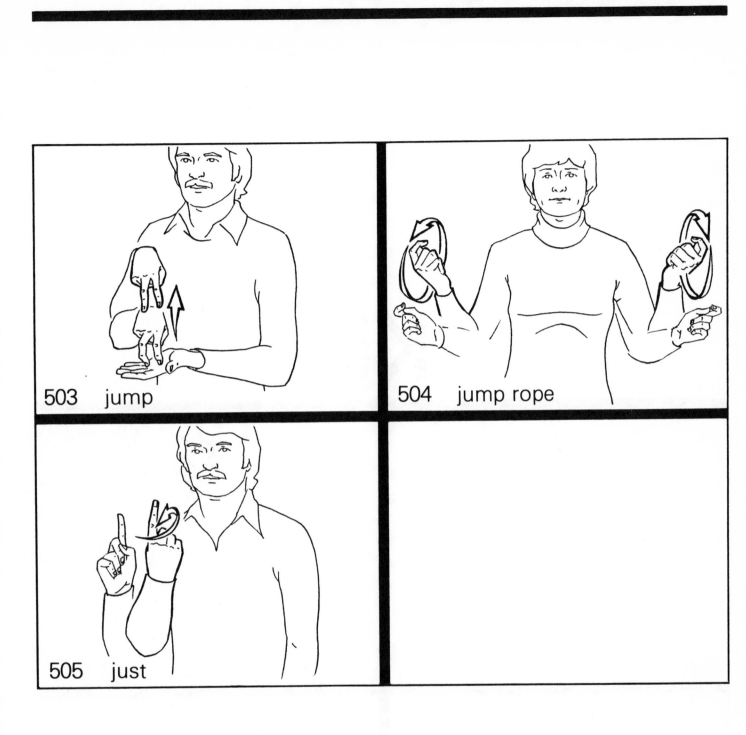

503   jump

504   jump rope

505   just

Kk

506   kangaroo

507   keep, take care of (DM)

508   kick

509   kind

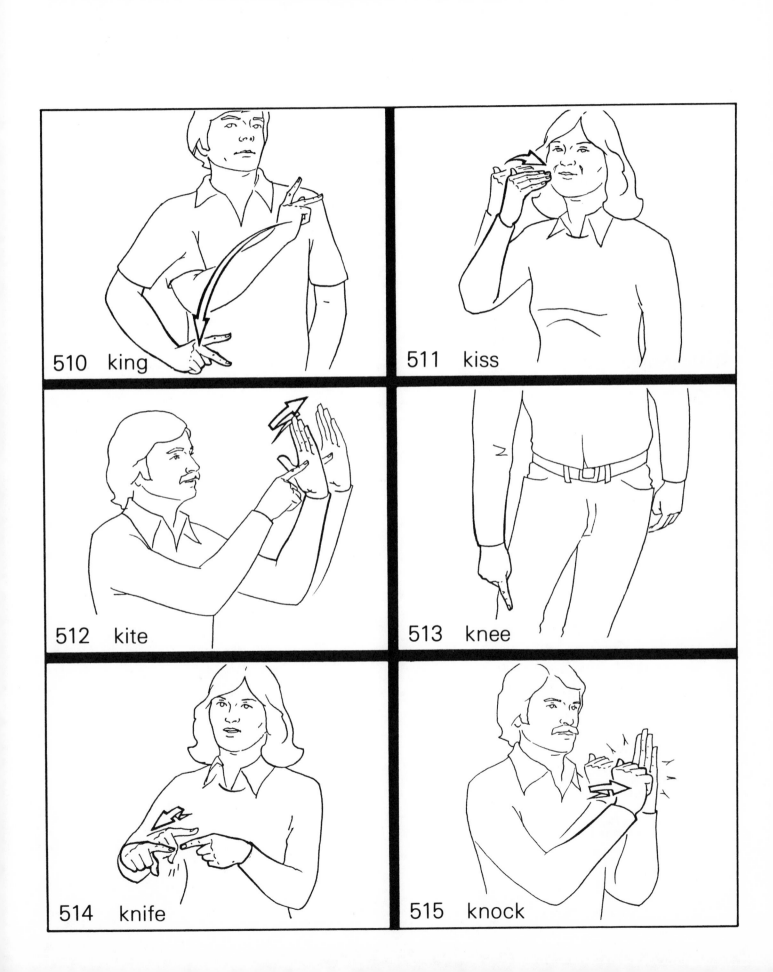

510 king

511 kiss

512 kite

513 knee

514 knife

515 knock

516 know

517 kitchen

LI

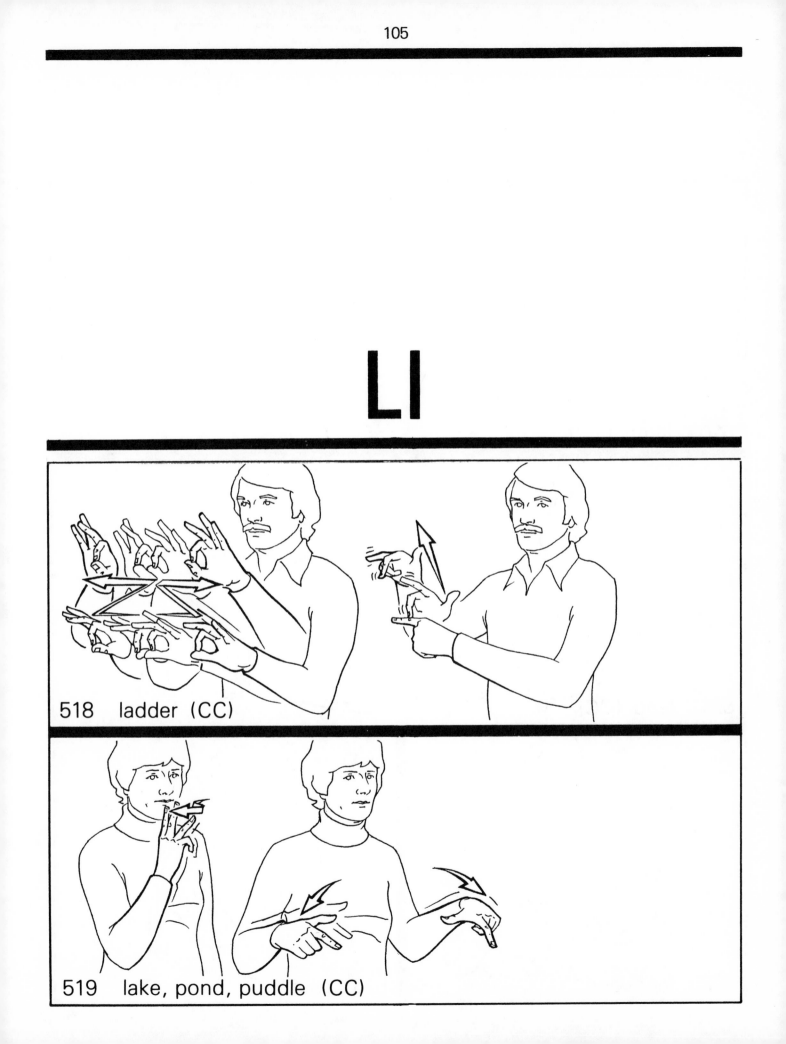

518   ladder (CC)

519   lake, pond, puddle (CC)

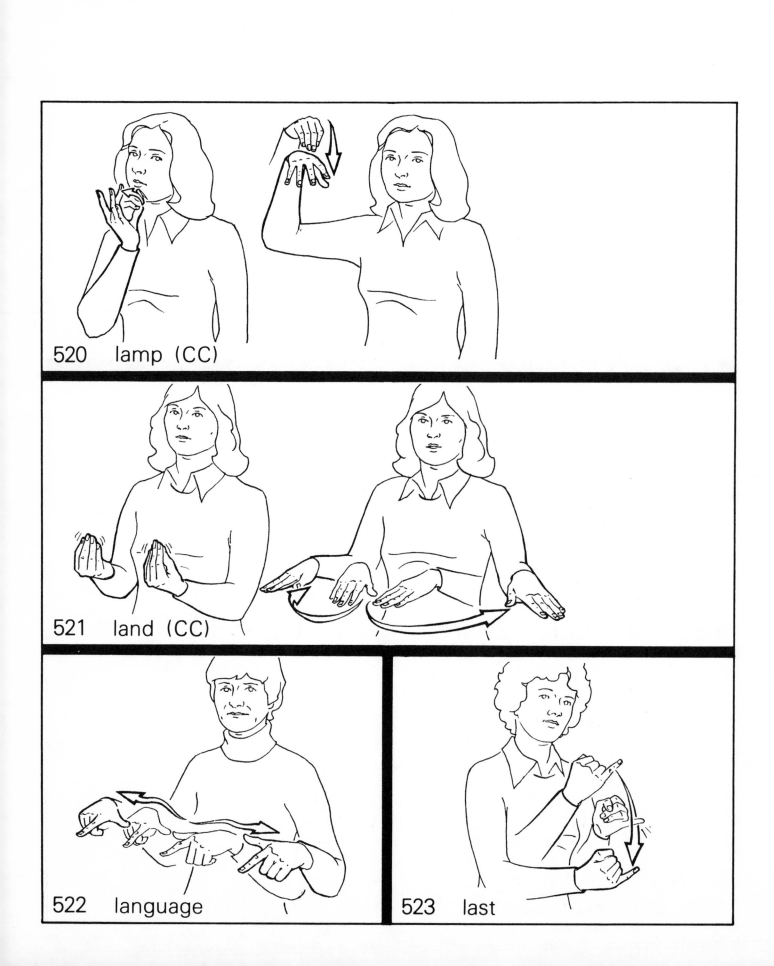

520   lamp (CC)

521   land (CC)

522   language

523   last

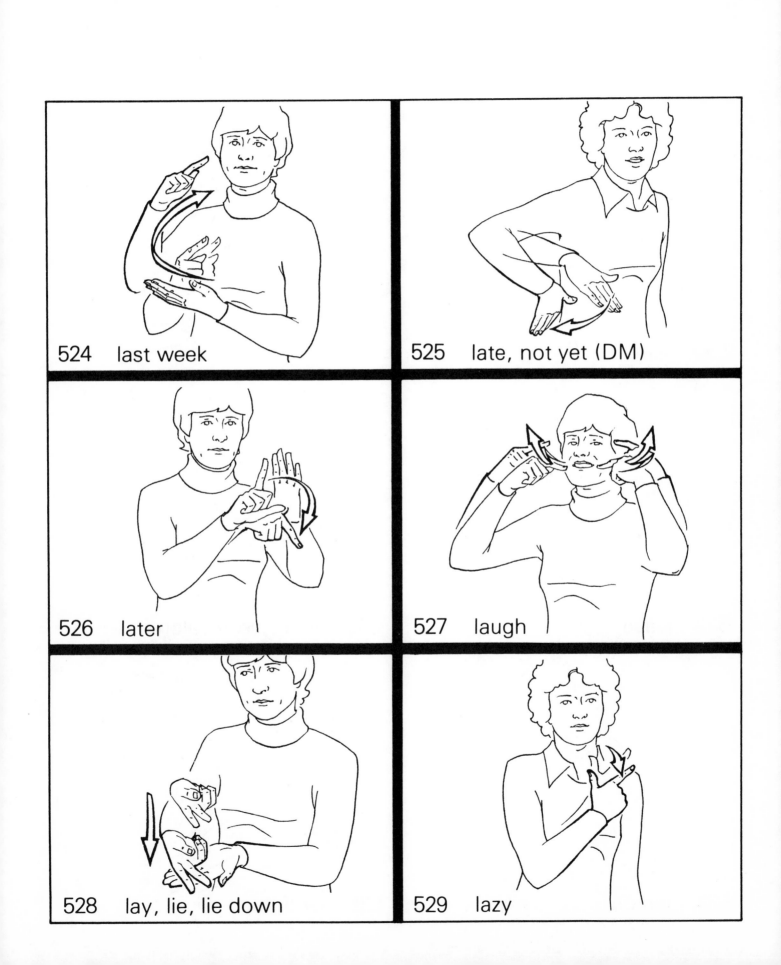

524   last week

525   late, not yet (DM)

526   later

527   laugh

528   lay, lie, lie down

529   lazy

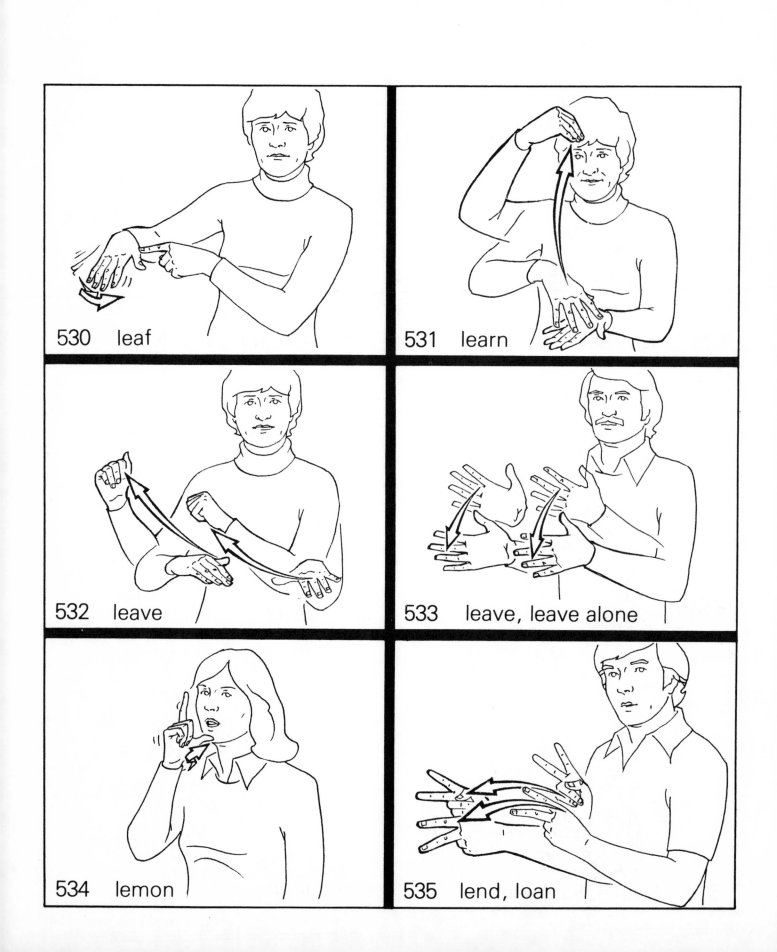

530   leaf

531   learn

532   leave

533   leave, leave alone

534   lemon

535   lend, loan

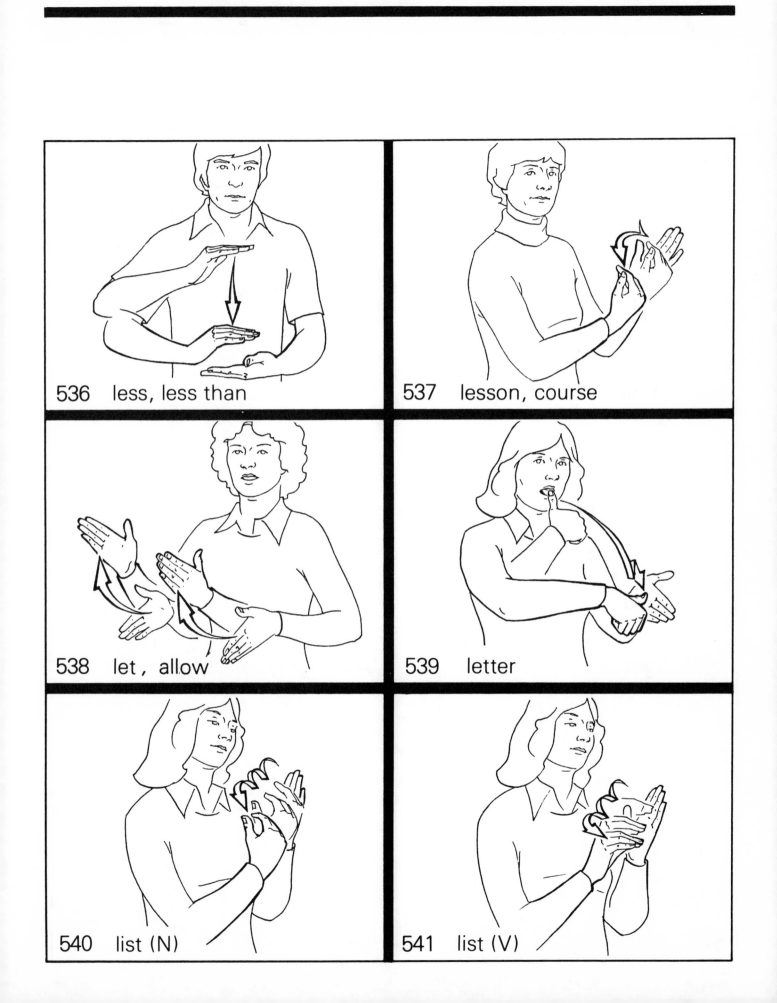

536   less, less than

537   lesson, course

538   let , allow

539   letter

540   list (N)

541   list (V)

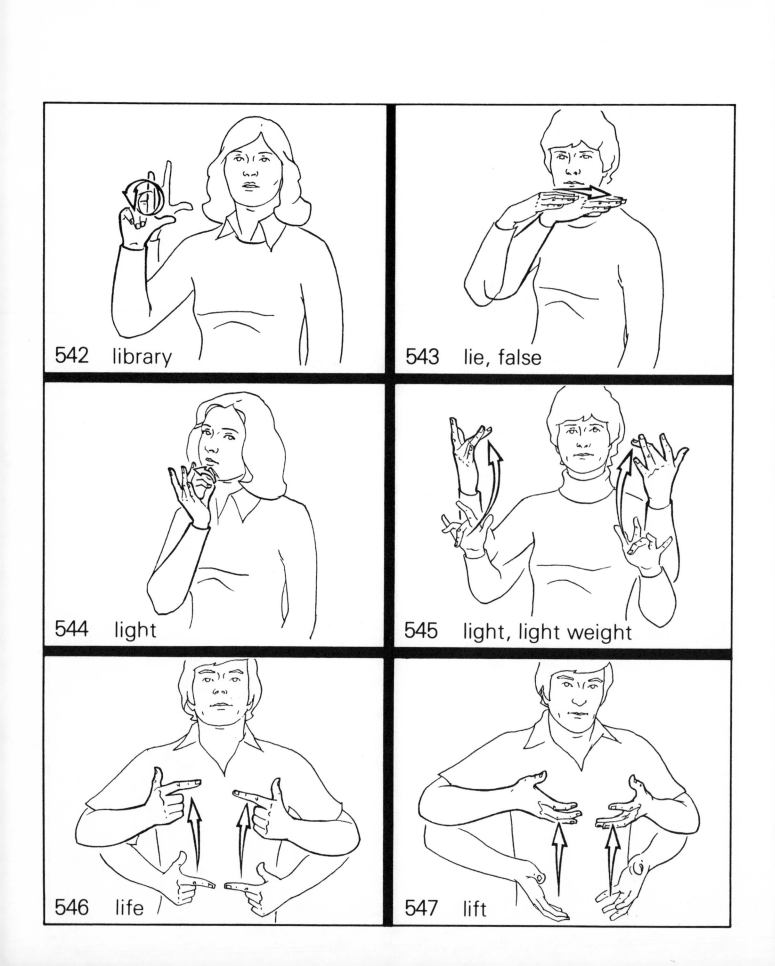

542 library

543 lie, false

544 light

545 light, light weight

546 life

547 lift

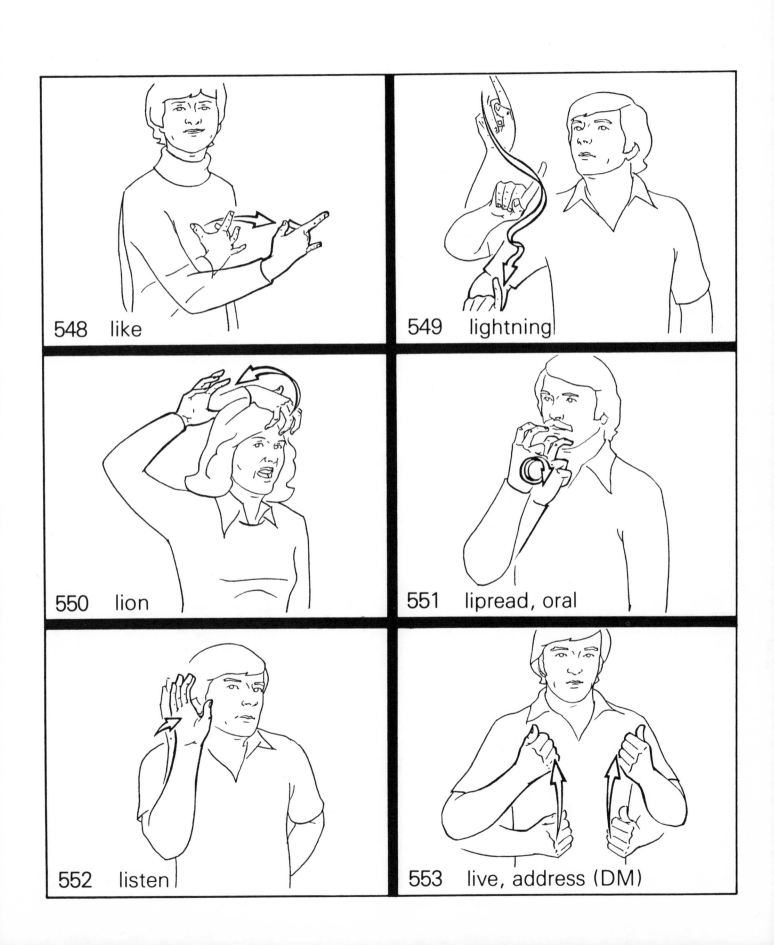

548 like

549 lightning

550 lion

551 lipread, oral

552 listen

553 live, address (DM)

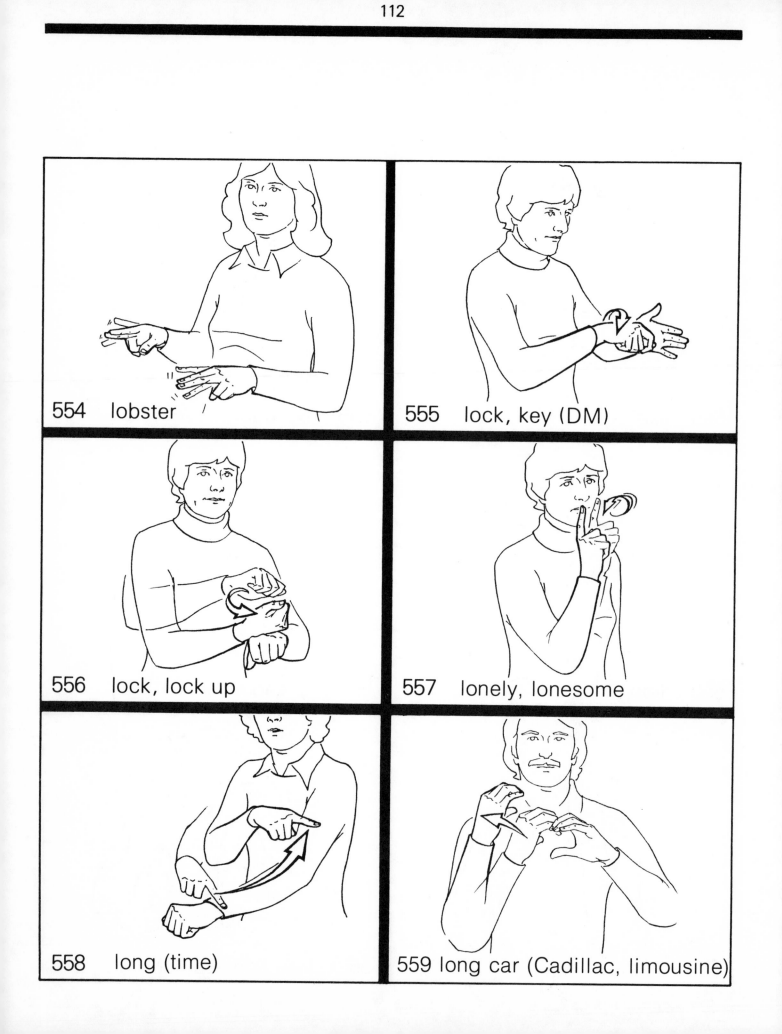

554   lobster

555   lock, key (DM)

556   lock, lock up

557   lonely, lonesome

558   long (time)

559 long car (Cadillac, limousine)

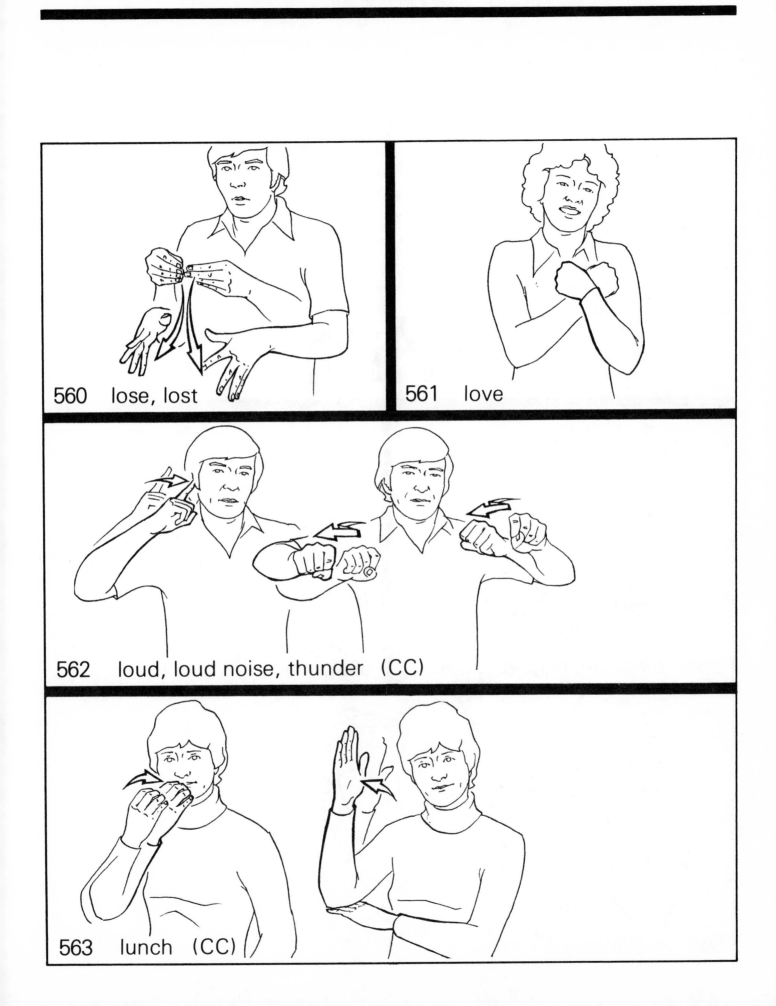

560   lose, lost

561   love

562   loud, loud noise, thunder (CC)

563   lunch (CC)

Mm

564   machine, engine, motor

565   mad

566   mailman (CC)

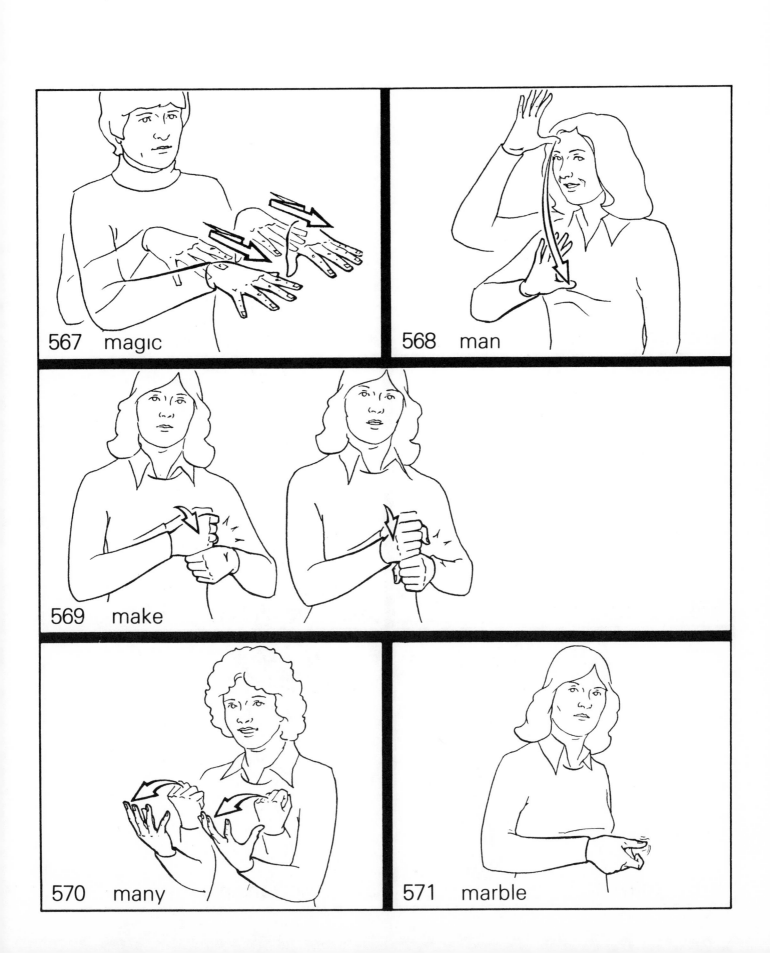

567 magic

568 man

569 make

570 many

571 marble

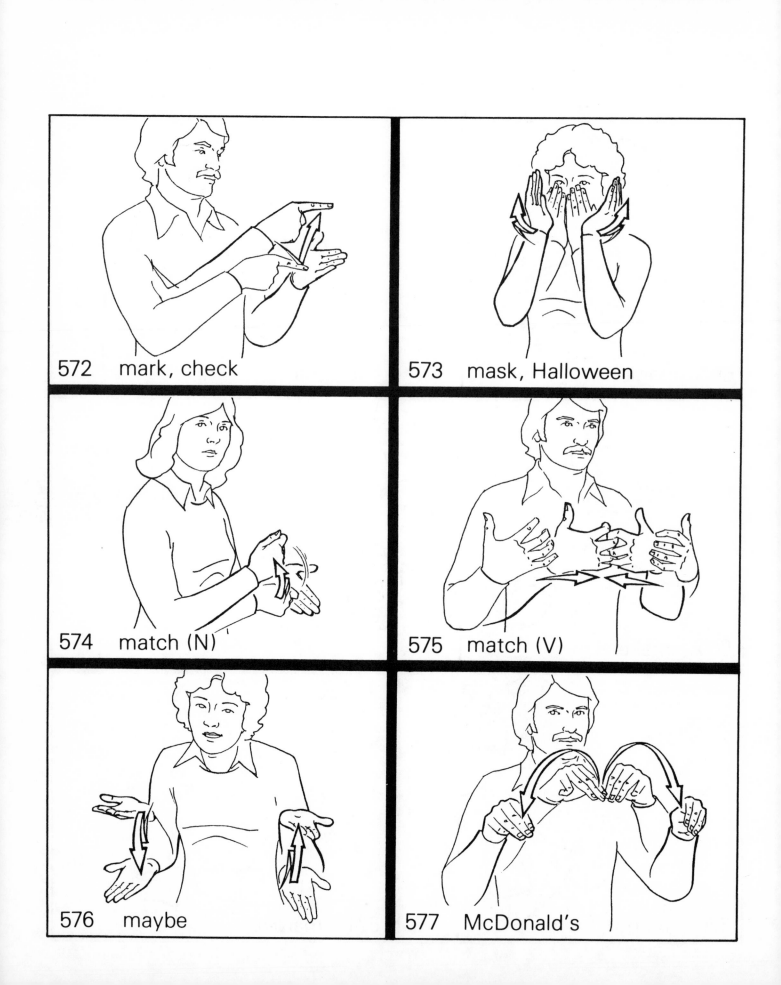

572 mark, check

573 mask, Halloween

574 match (N)

575 match (V)

576 maybe

577 McDonald's

578　me

579　measles, freckles

580　mean, meaning

581　meat

582　mechanic, plumber

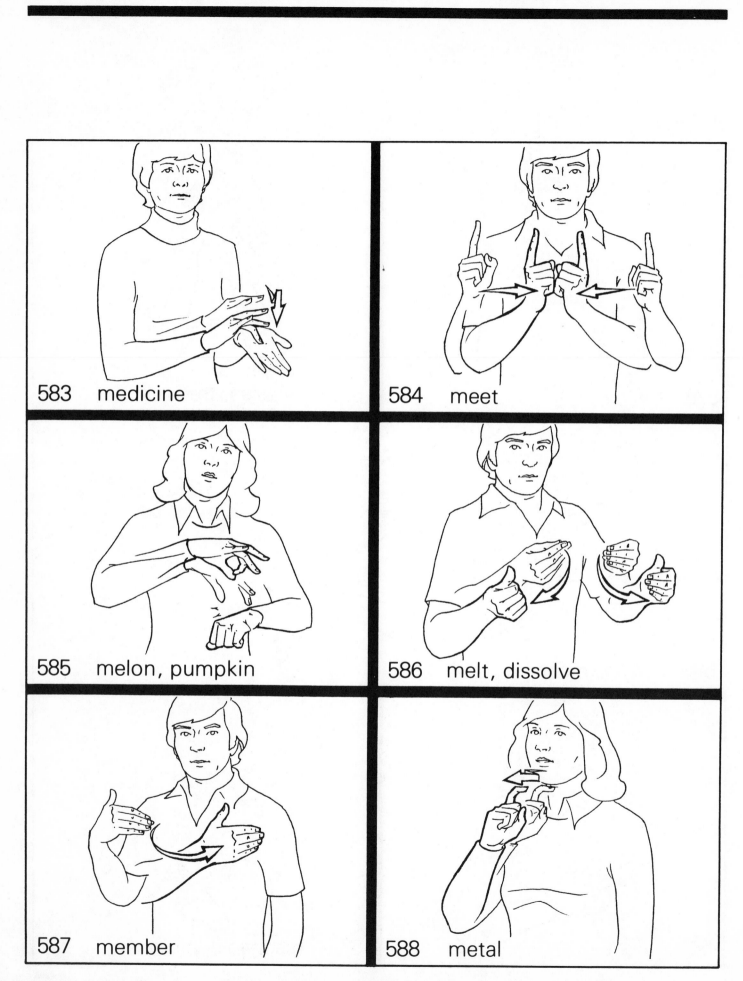

583 medicine

584 meet

585 melon, pumpkin

586 melt, dissolve

587 member

588 metal

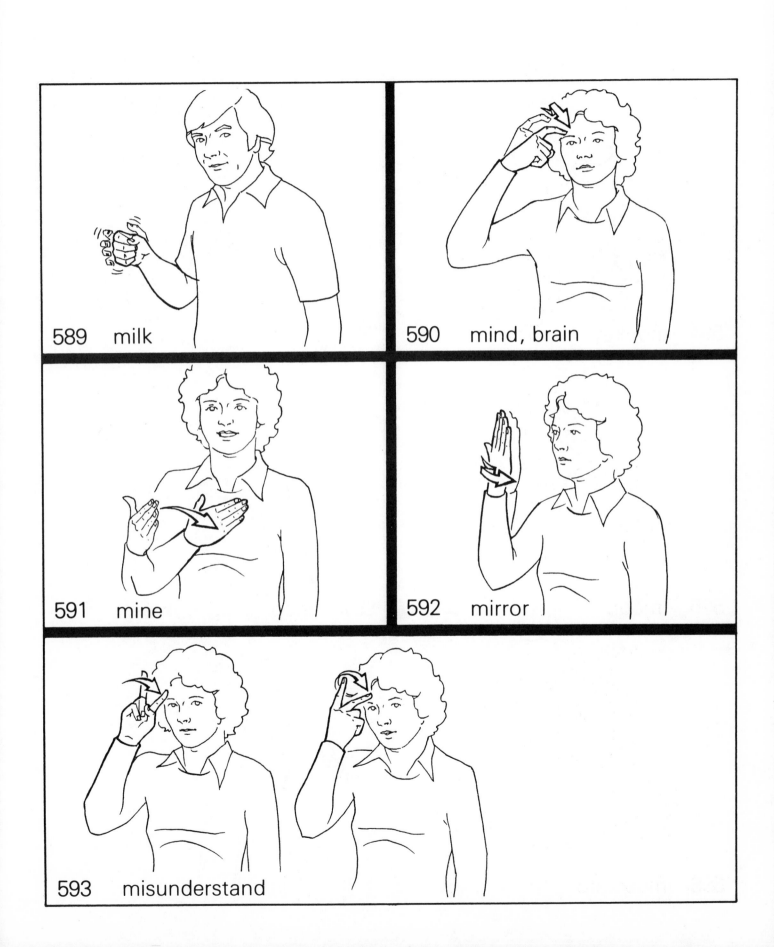

589   milk

590   mind, brain

591   mine

592   mirror

593   misunderstand

594 monkey

595 month

596 moon

597 mop

598 mosquito

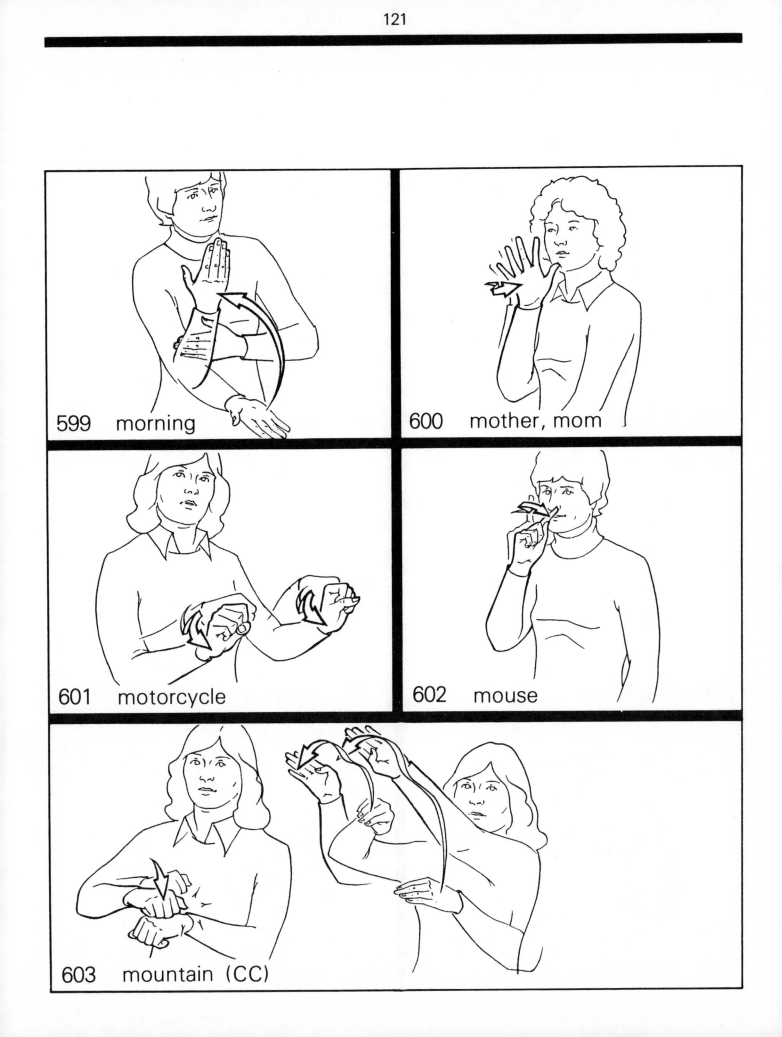

599　morning

600　mother, mom

601　motorcycle

602　mouse

603　mountain (CC)

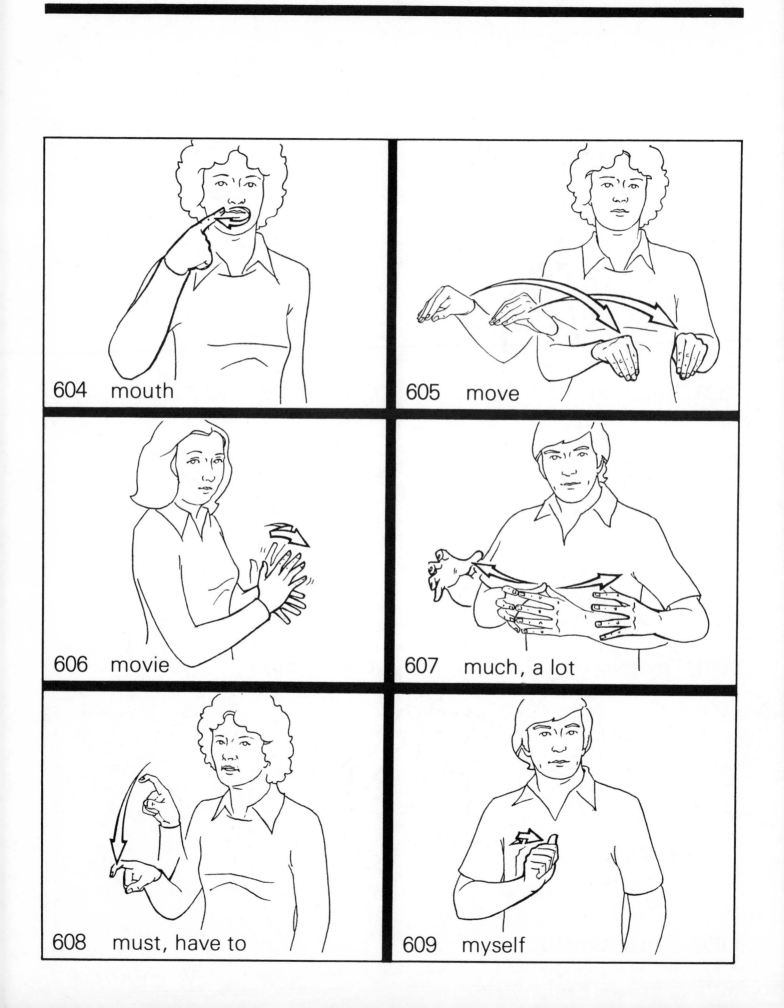

604 mouth

605 move

606 movie

607 much, a lot

608 must, have to

609 myself

Nn

610 name

611 napkin

612 nap (CC)

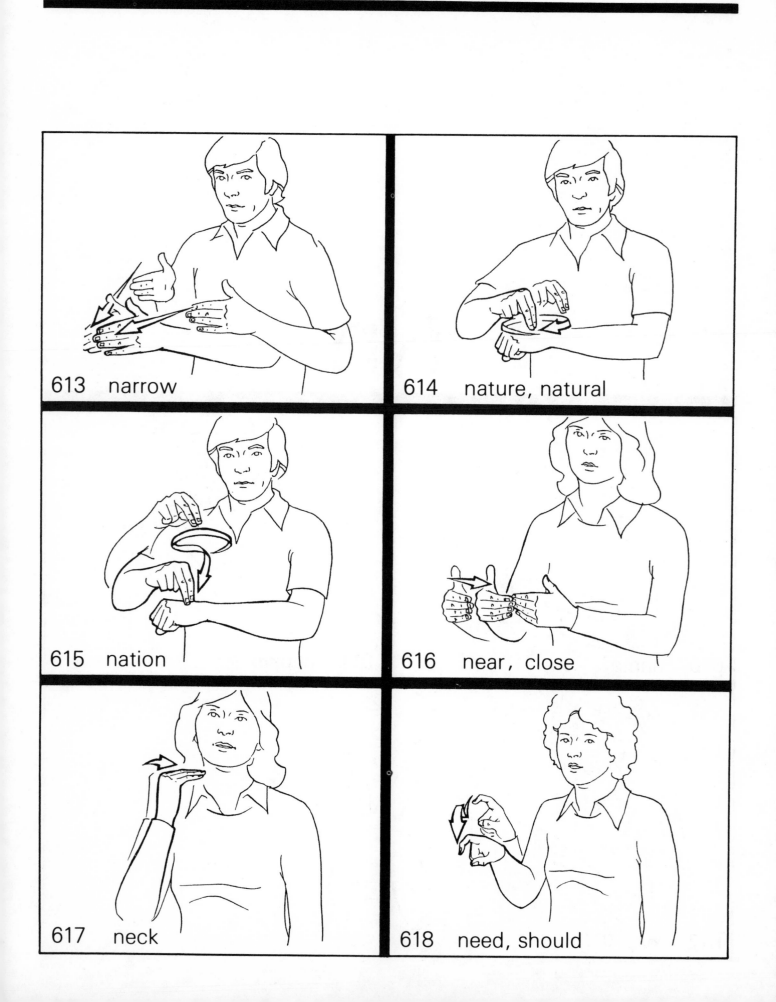

613 narrow

614 nature, natural

615 nation

616 near, close

617 neck

618 need, should

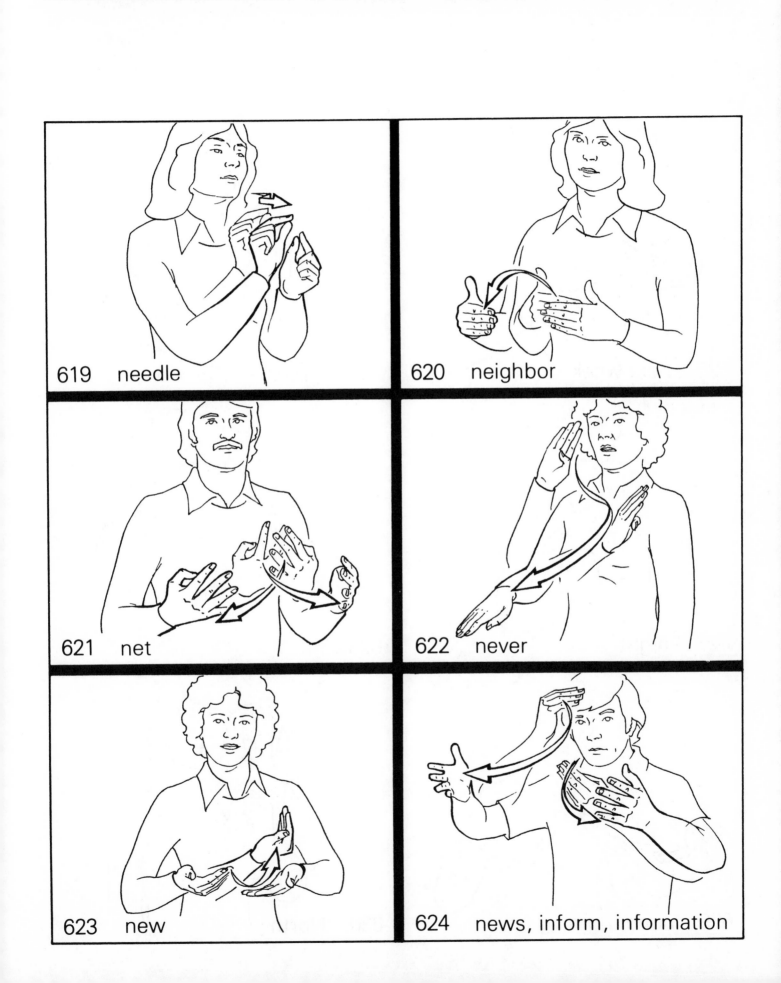

619 needle

620 neighbor

621 net

622 never

623 new

624 news, inform, information

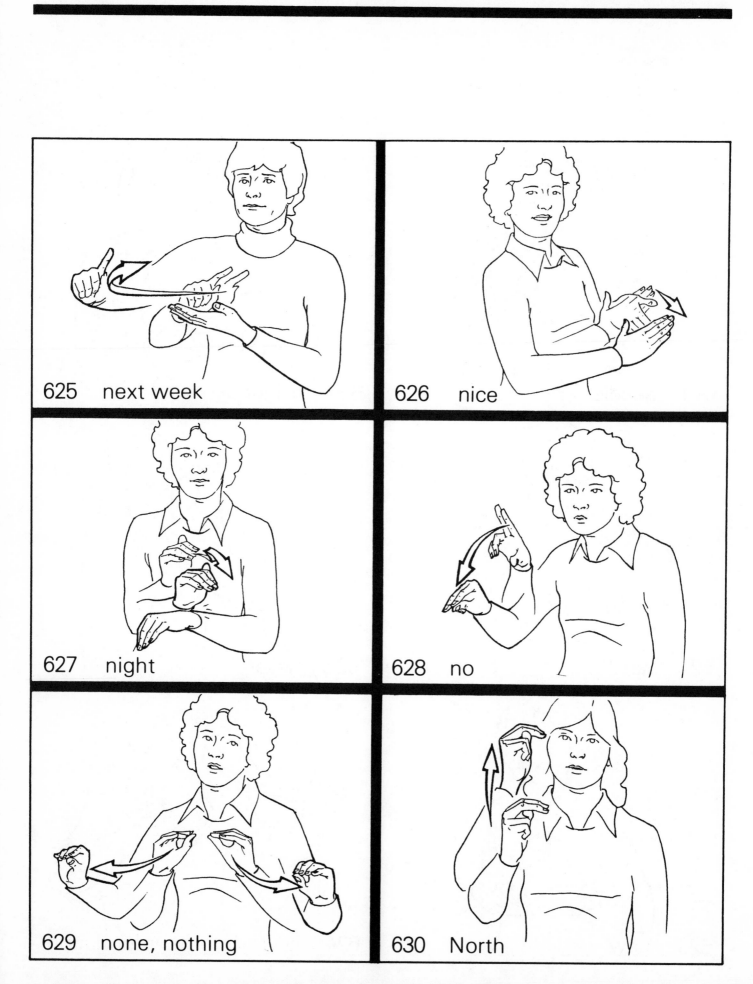

625　next week

626　nice

627　night

628　no

629　none, nothing

630　North

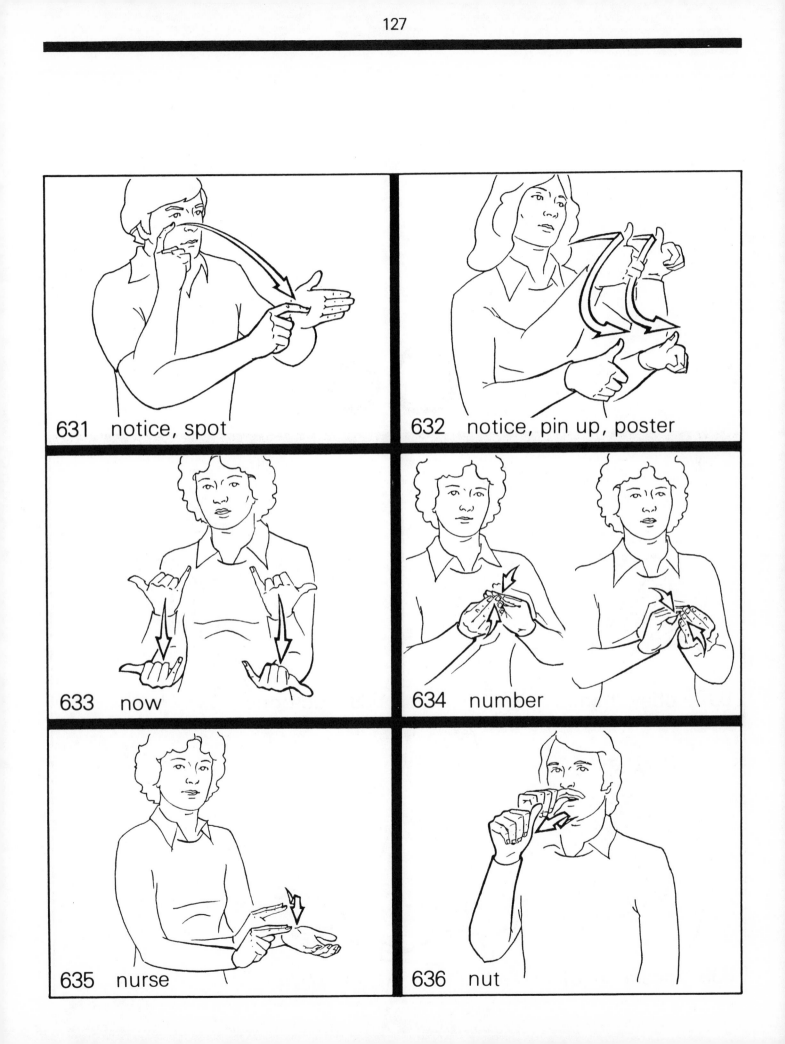

631 notice, spot

632 notice, pin up, poster

633 now

634 number

635 nurse

636 nut

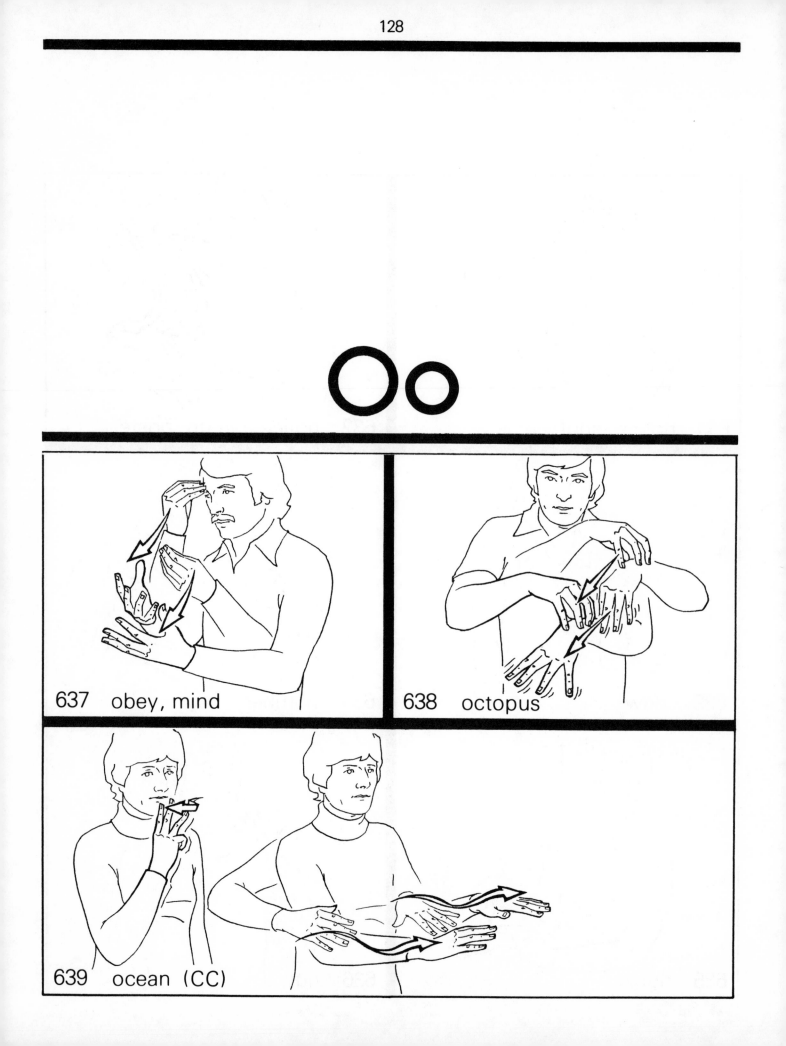

637 obey, mind

638 octopus

639 ocean (CC)

129

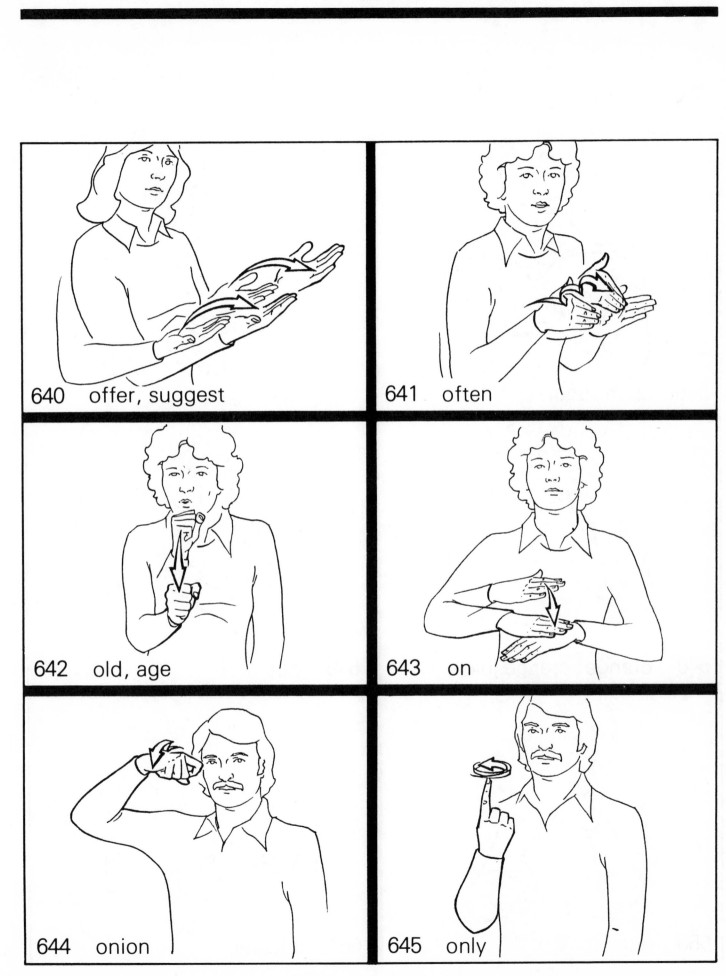

640 offer, suggest

641 often

642 old, age

643 on

644 onion

645 only

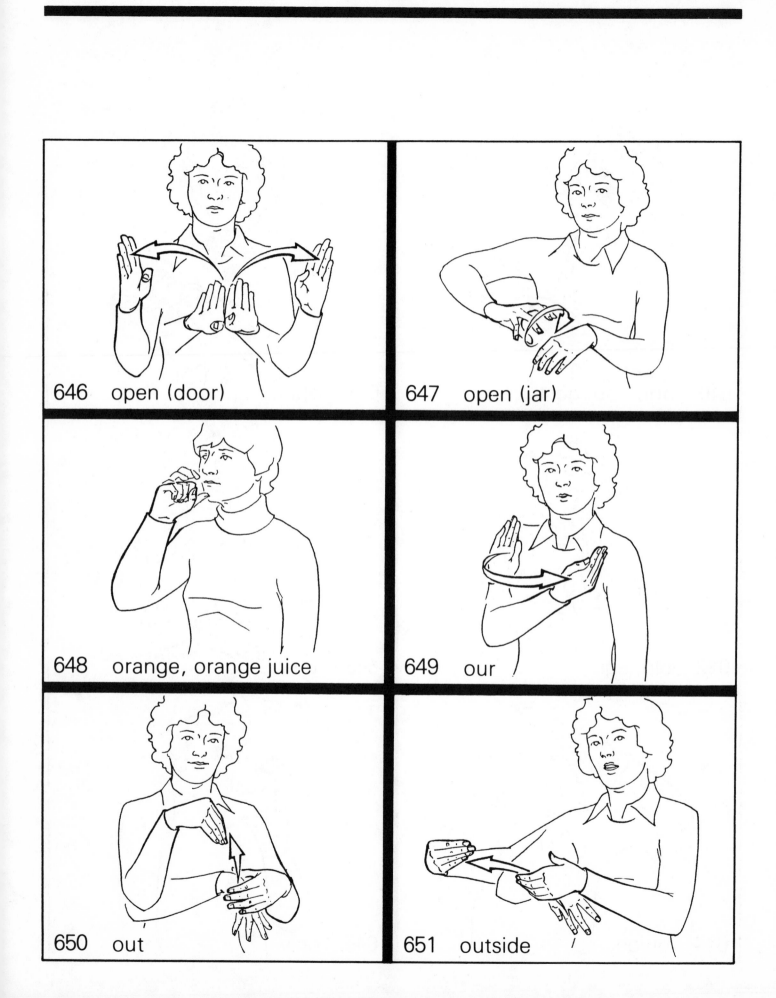

646 open (door)

647 open (jar)

648 orange, orange juice

649 our

650 out

651 outside

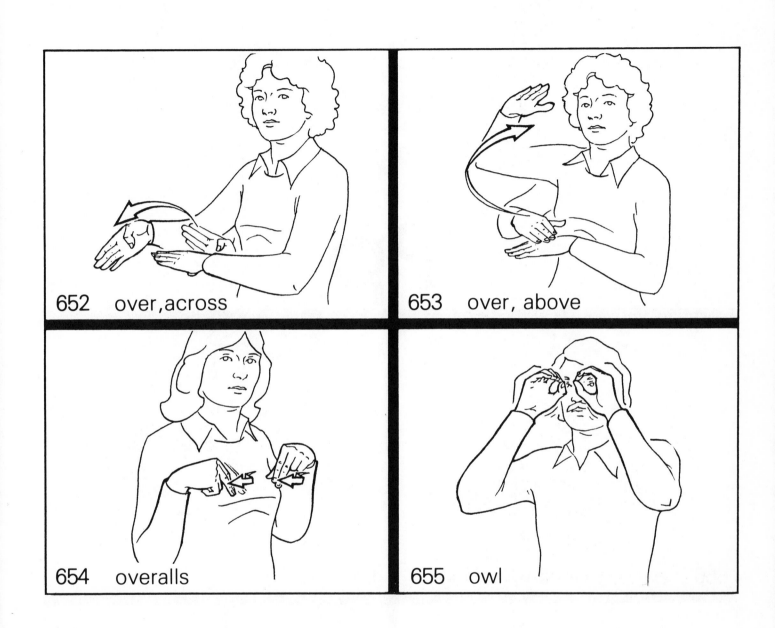

652 over, across

653 over, above

654 overalls

655 owl

Pp

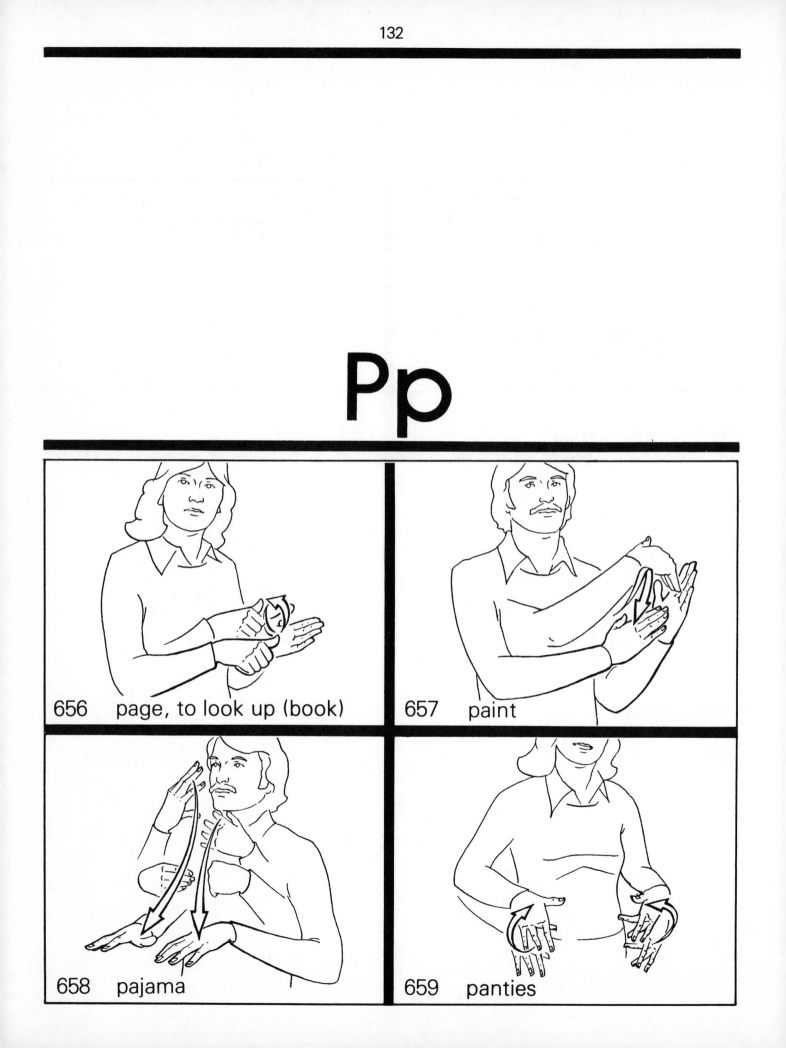

656   page, to look up (book)

657   paint

658   pajama

659   panties

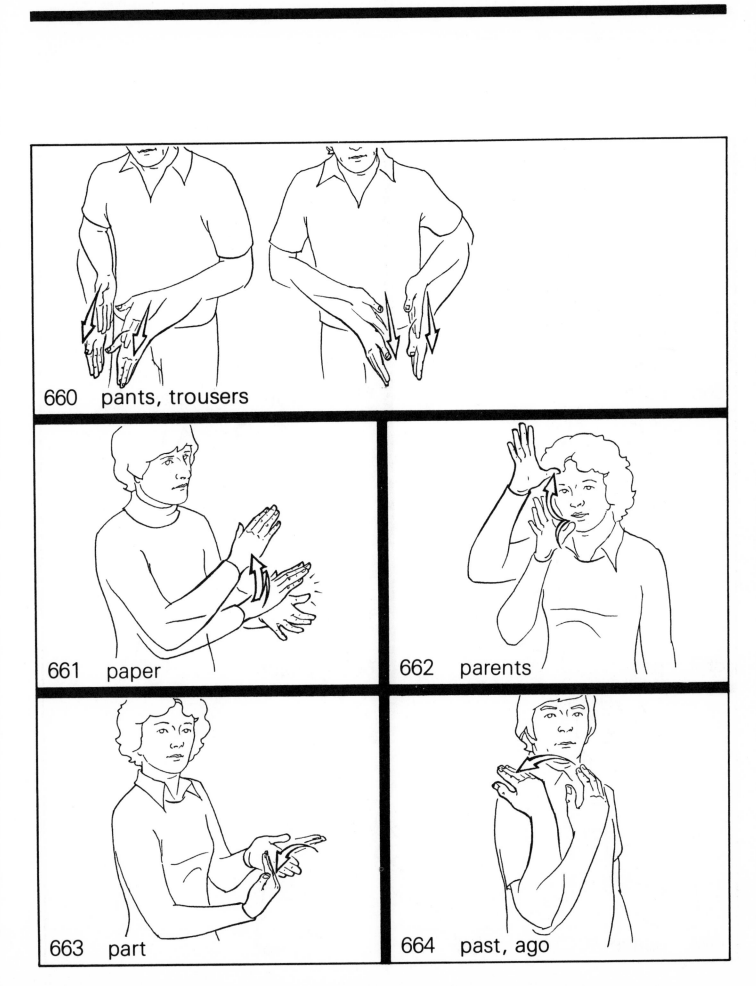

660 pants, trousers

661 paper

662 parents

663 part

664 past, ago

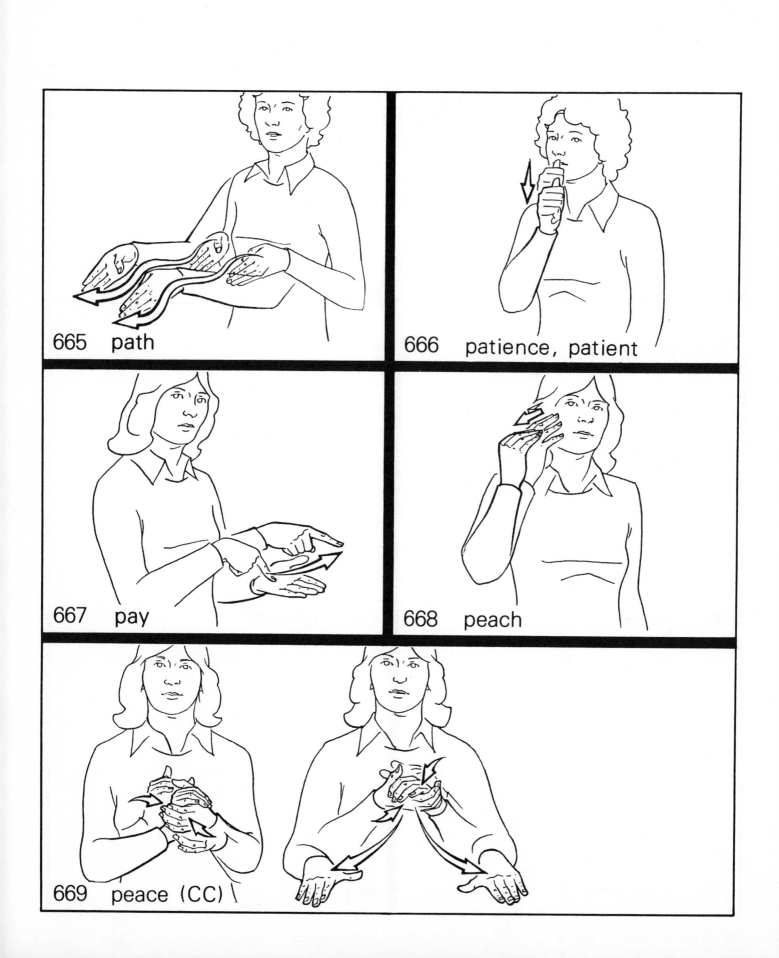

665   path

666   patience, patient

667   pay

668   peach

669   peace (CC)

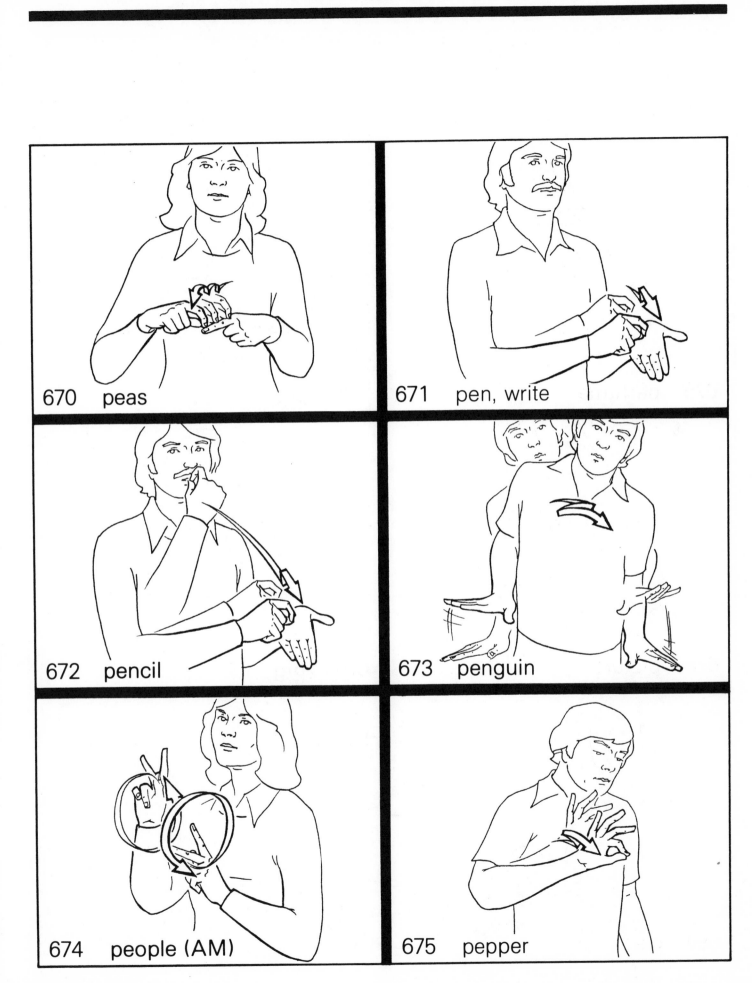

670   peas

671   pen, write

672   pencil

673   penguin

674   people (AM)

675   pepper

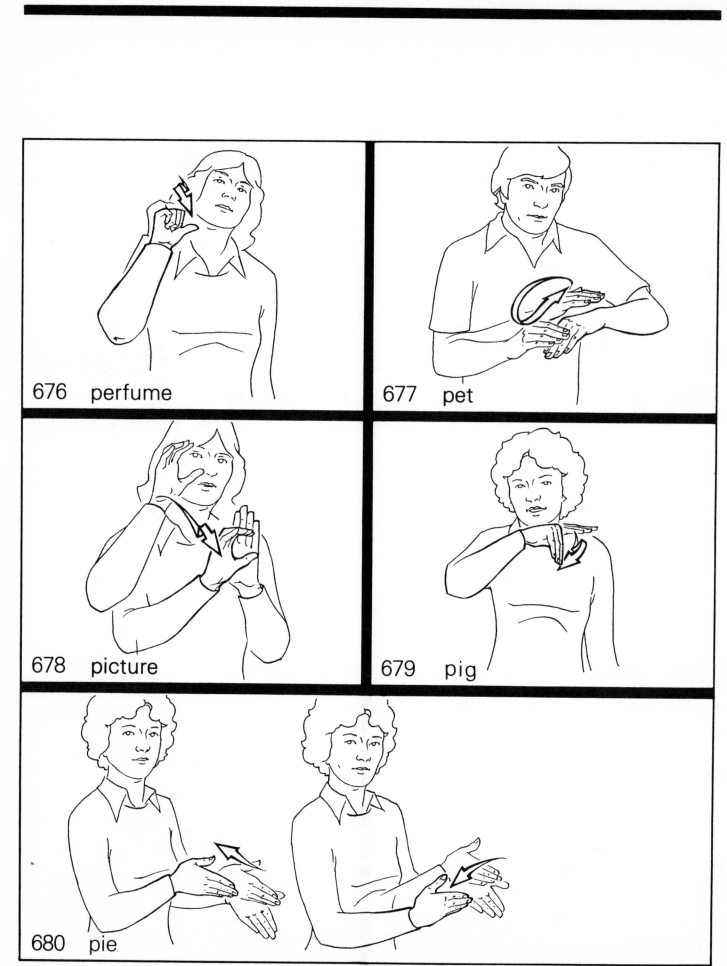

676　perfume

677　pet

678　picture

679　pig

680　pie

681 pink

682 pipe

683 pity

684 plan

685 plant (V)

686 plate

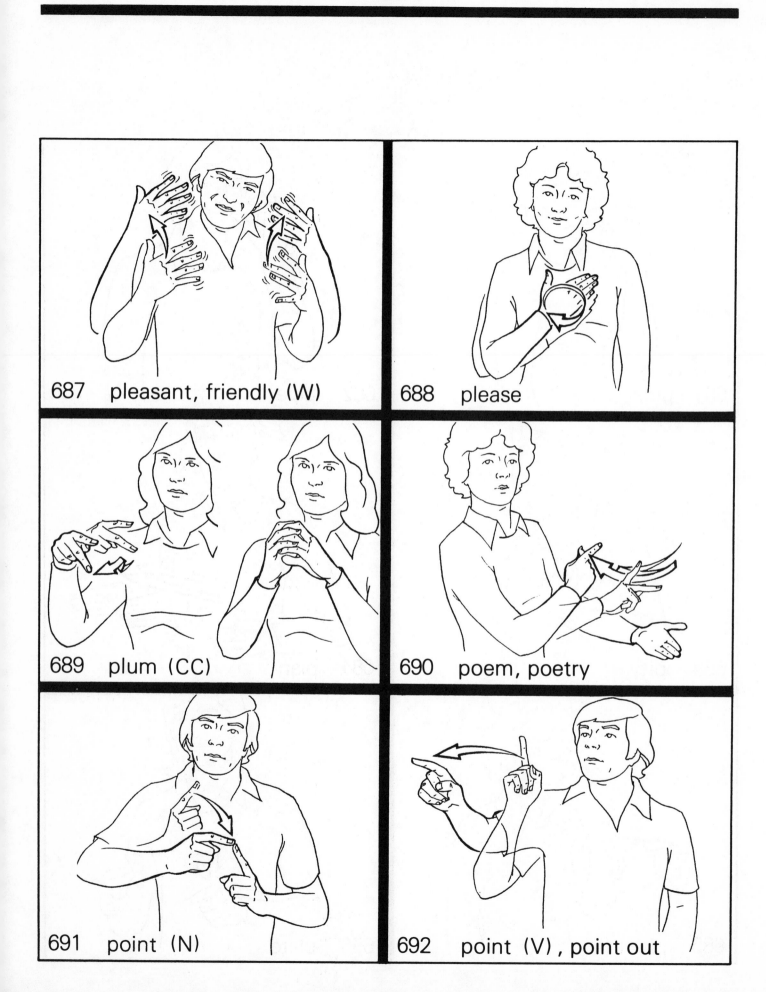

687   pleasant, friendly (W)

688   please

689   plum (CC)

690   poem, poetry

691   point (N)

692   point (V) , point out

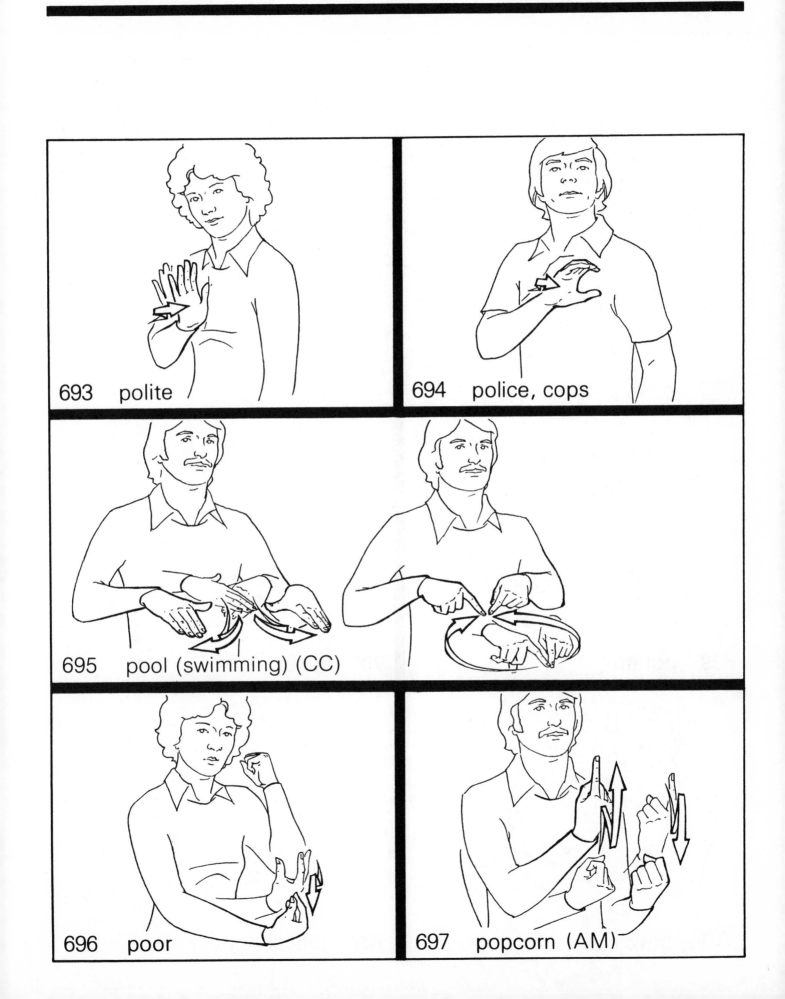

693   polite

694   police, cops

695   pool (swimming) (CC)

696   poor

697   popcorn (AM)

698　　post, pole　(CC)

699　　potato

700　　pour

701　　power

702　　practice, train (V)

703   pray

704   pretty

705   press, pressure (DM)

706   pretend, make believe

707   pretend, fool

708   print (V), newspaper (DM)

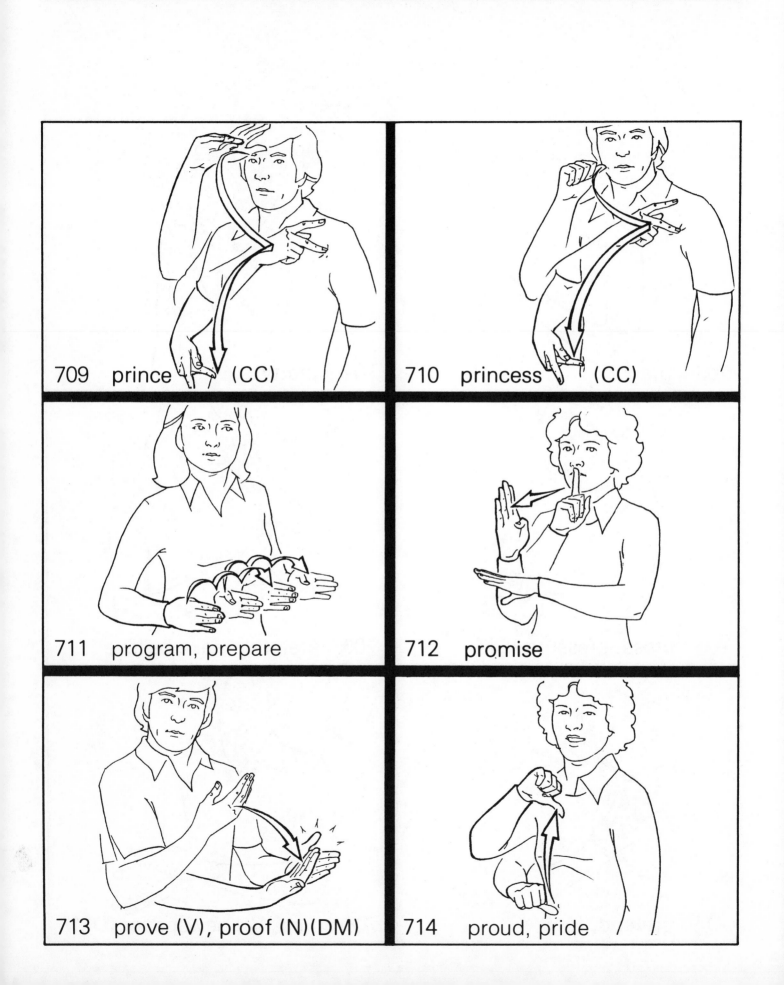

709   prince   (CC)

710   princess   (CC)

711   program, prepare

712   promise

713   prove (V), proof (N)(DM)

714   proud, pride

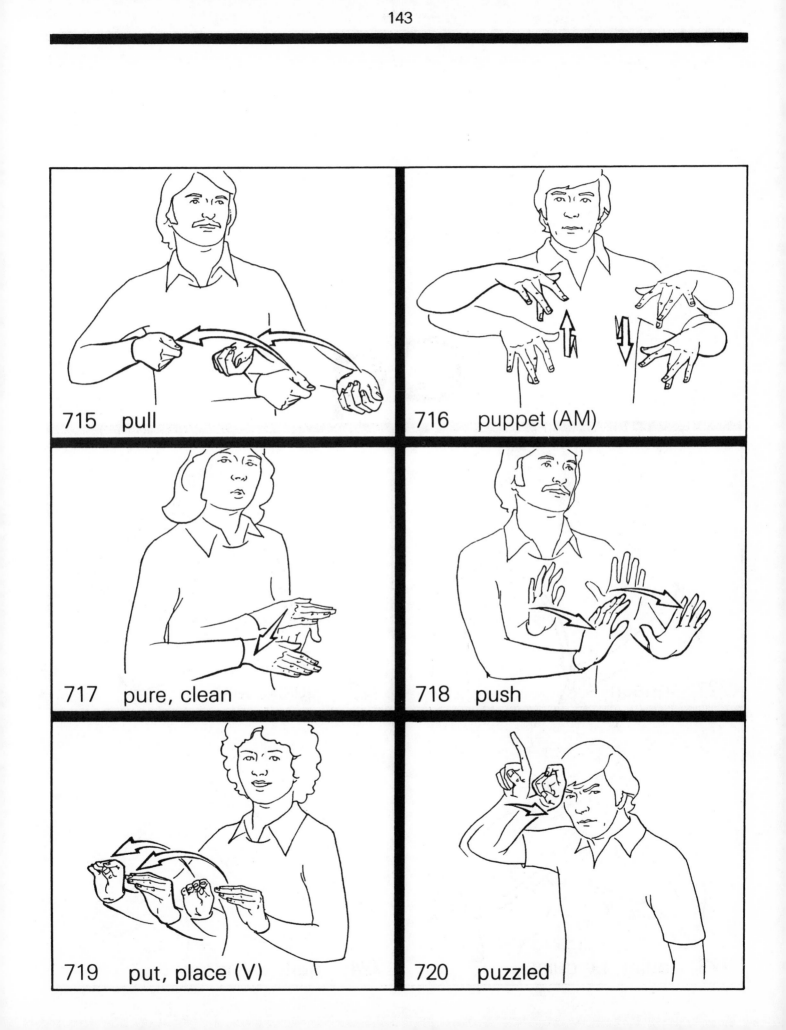

715 pull

716 puppet (AM)

717 pure, clean

718 push

719 put, place (V)

720 puzzled

Qq

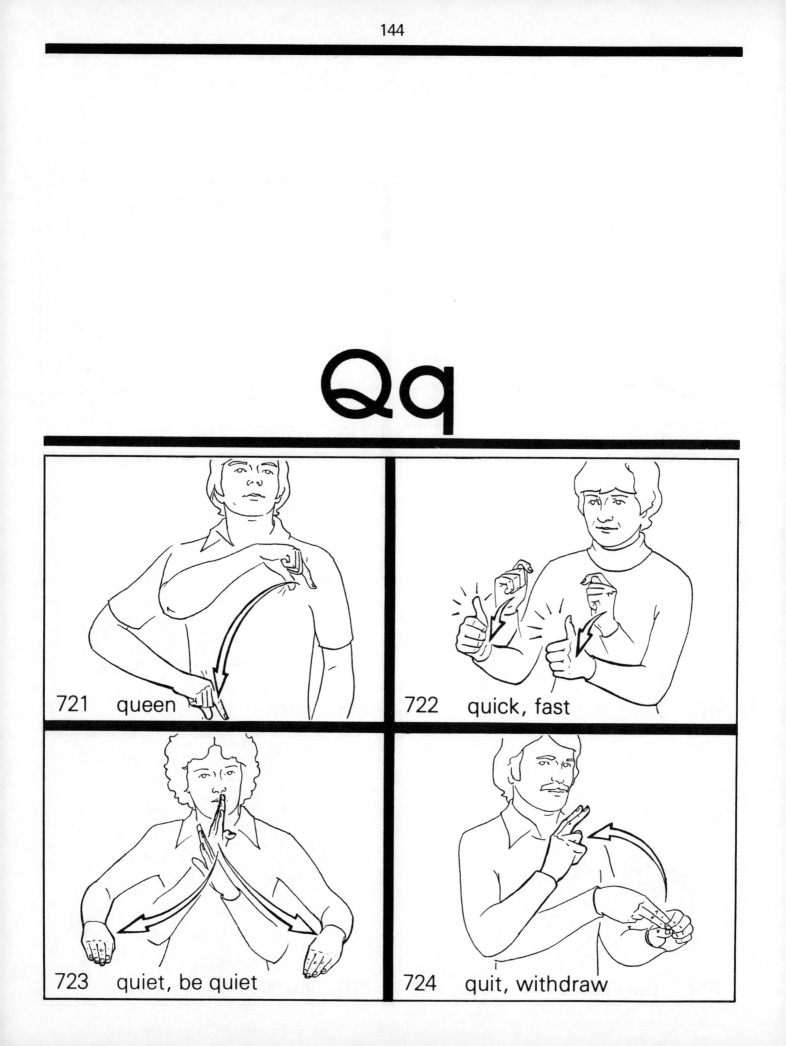

721   queen

722   quick, fast

723   quiet, be quiet

724   quit, withdraw

Rr

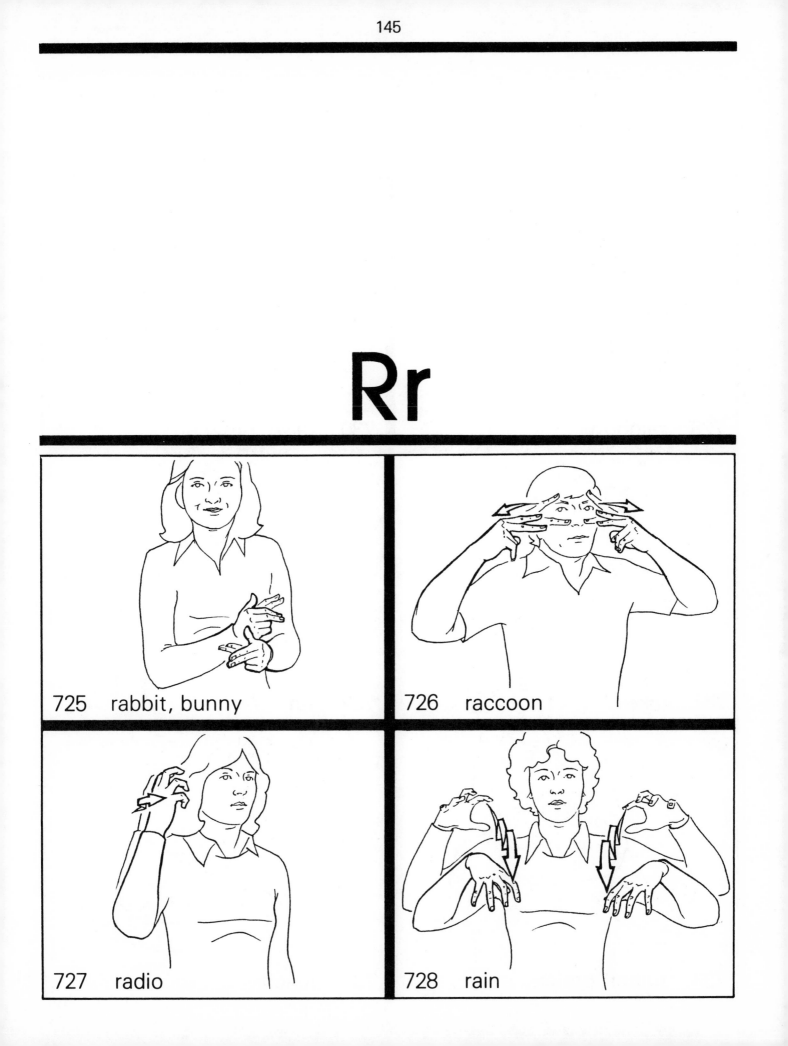

725   rabbit, bunny

726   raccoon

727   radio

728   rain

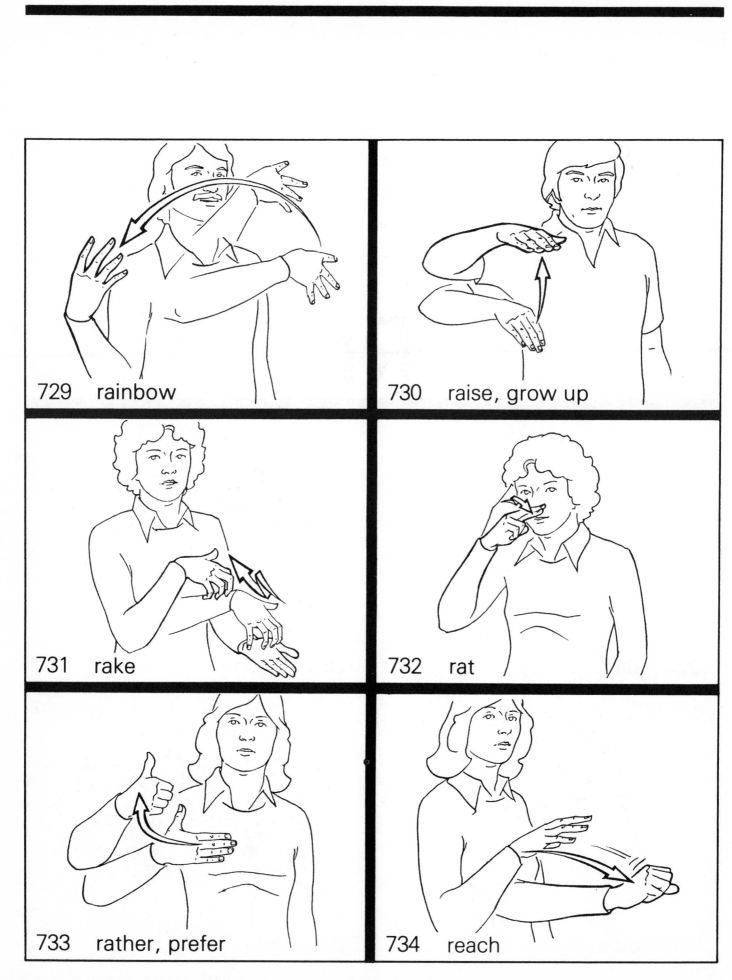

729 rainbow

730 raise, grow up

731 rake

732 rat

733 rather, prefer

734 reach

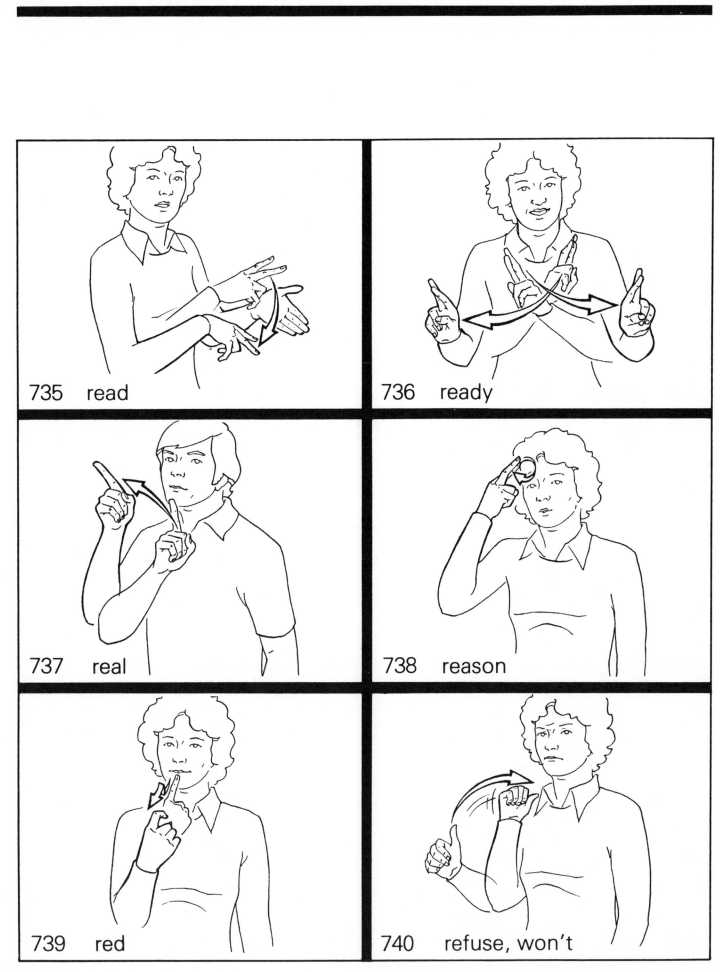

735 read

736 ready

737 real

738 reason

739 red

740 refuse, won't

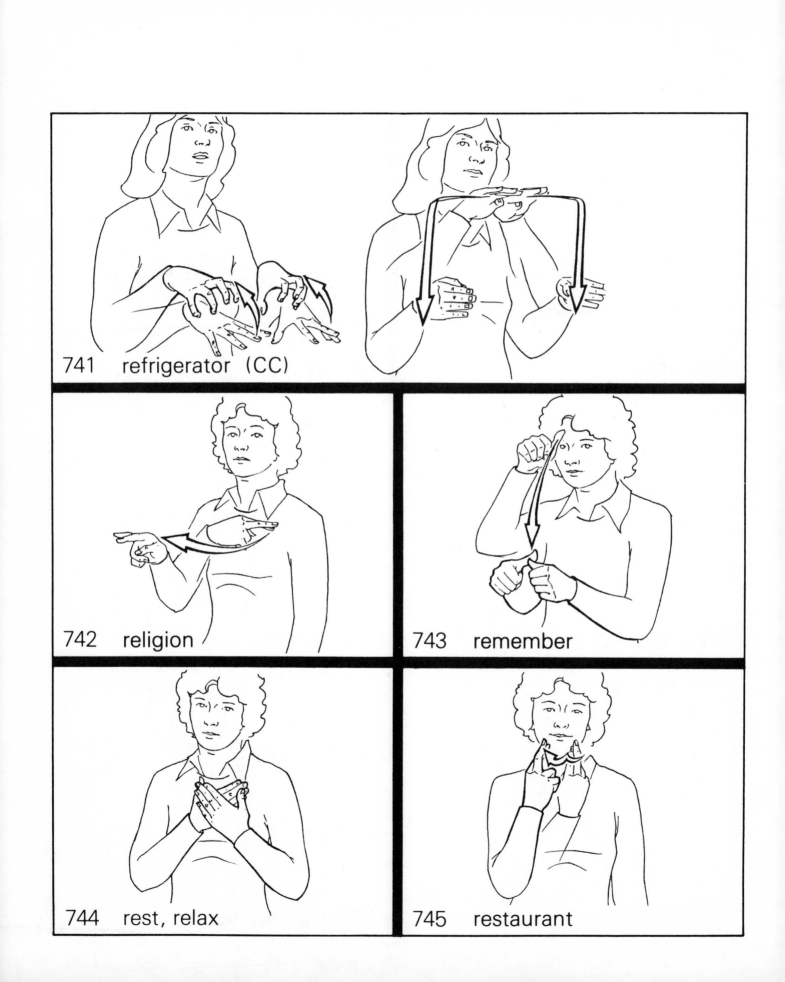

741 refrigerator (CC)

742 religion

743 remember

744 rest, relax

745 restaurant

746 rich, wealth

747 ride (horse)

748 ride (vehicle)

749 right (civil, legal), alright (DM)

750 right, correct

751 right (direction)

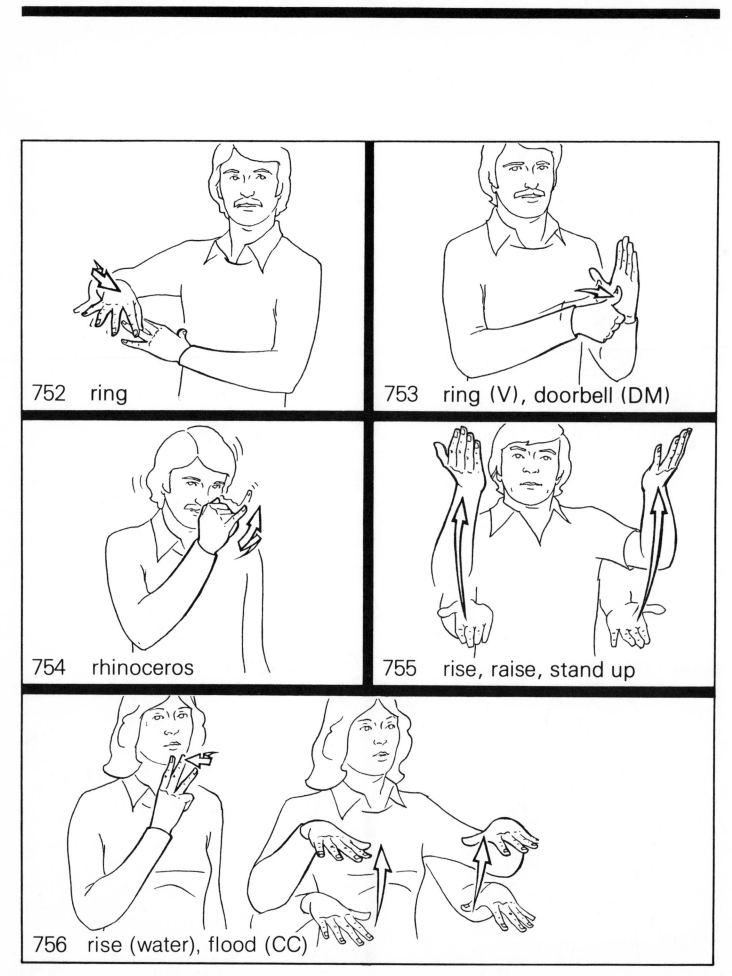

752 ring

753 ring (V), doorbell (DM)

754 rhinoceros

755 rise, raise, stand up

756 rise (water), flood (CC)

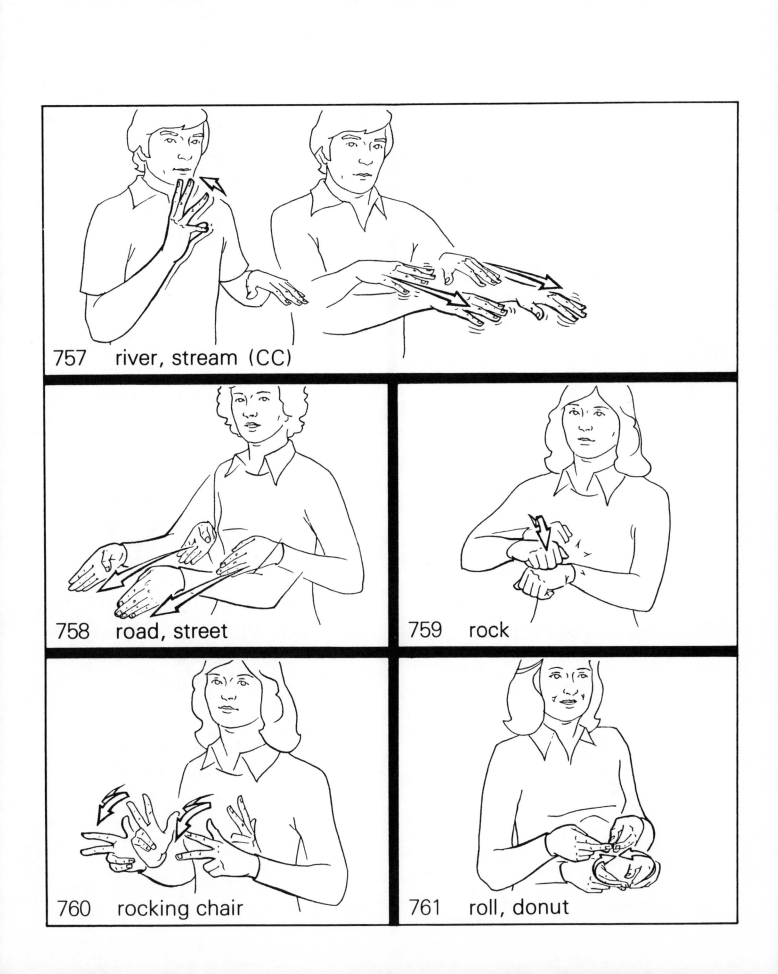

757 river, stream (CC)

758 road, street

759 rock

760 rocking chair

761 roll, donut

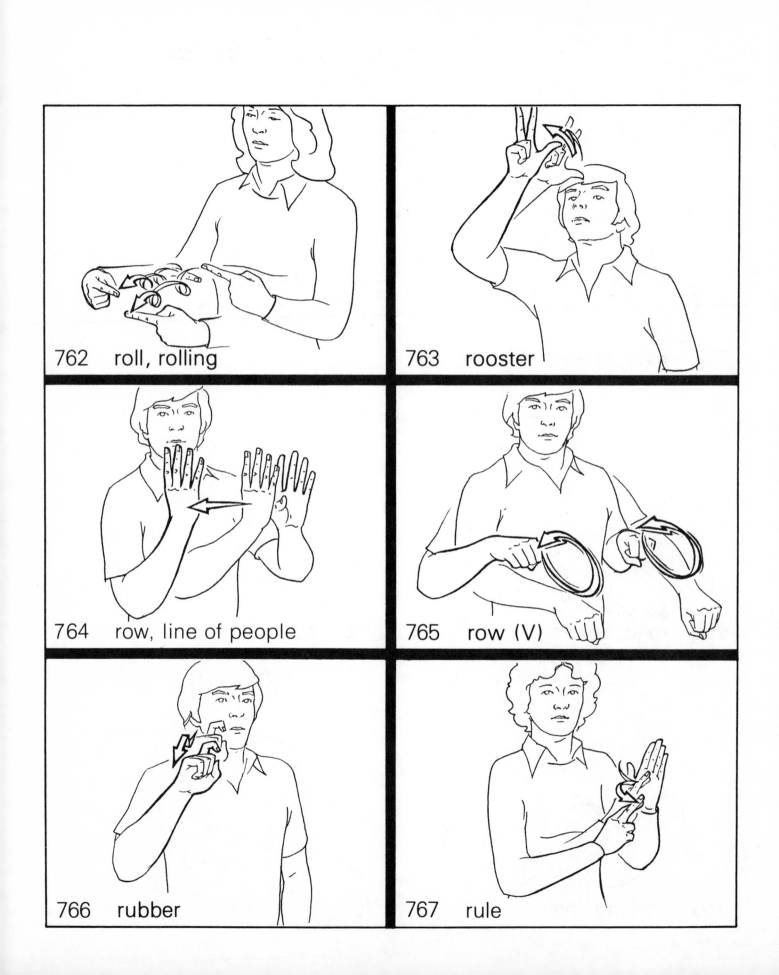

762   roll, rolling

763   rooster

764   row, line of people

765   row (V)

766   rubber

767   rule

153

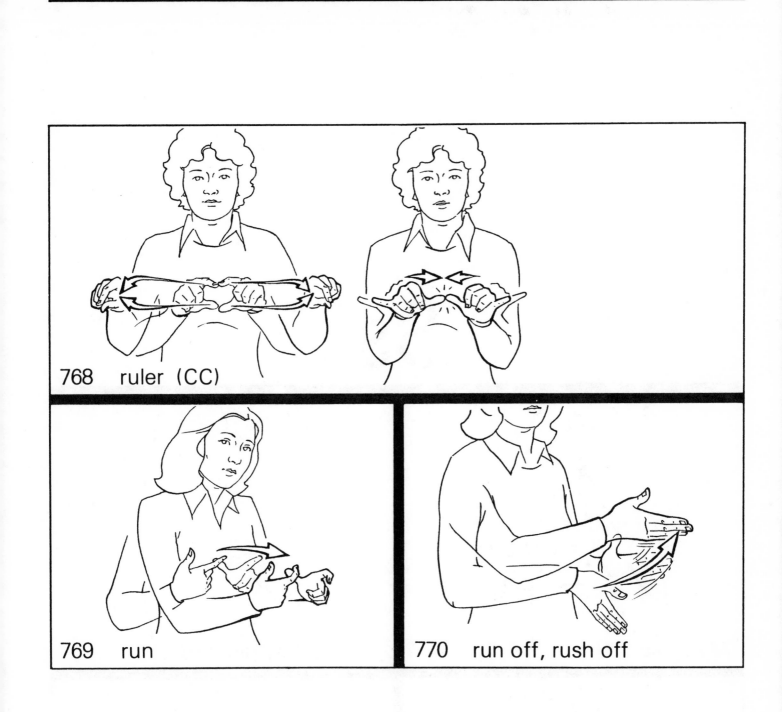

768   ruler (CC)

769   run

770   run off, rush off

Ss

771   sad

772   safety pin, brooch

773   sailboat

774   salt

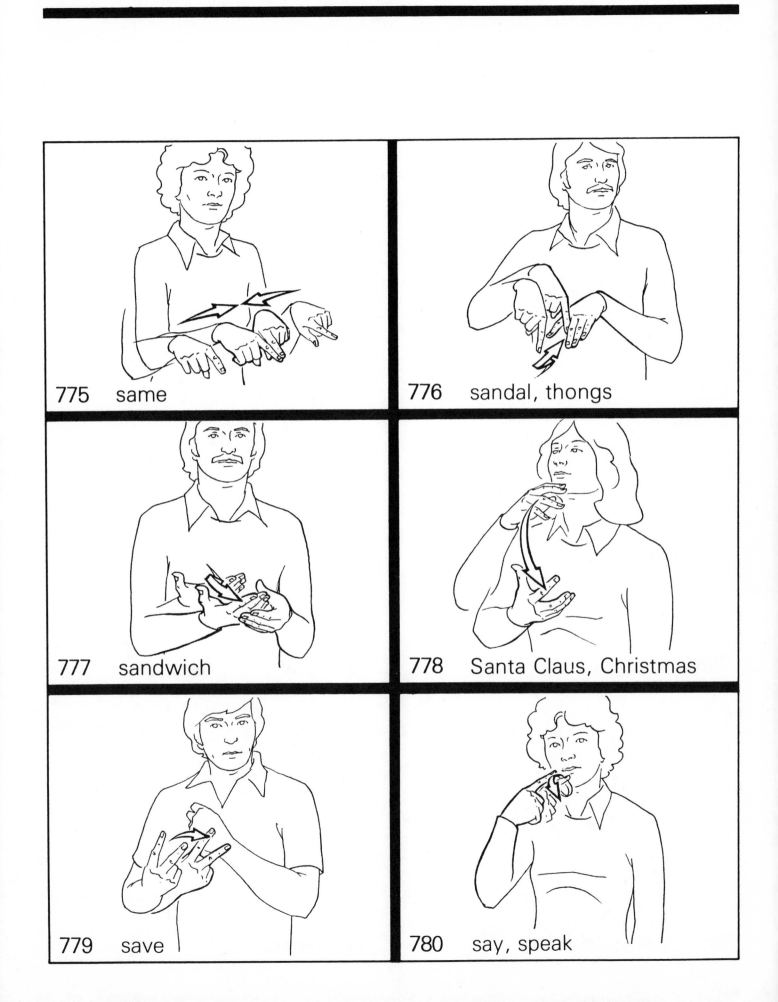

775   same

776   sandal, thongs

777   sandwich

778   Santa Claus, Christmas

779   save

780   say, speak

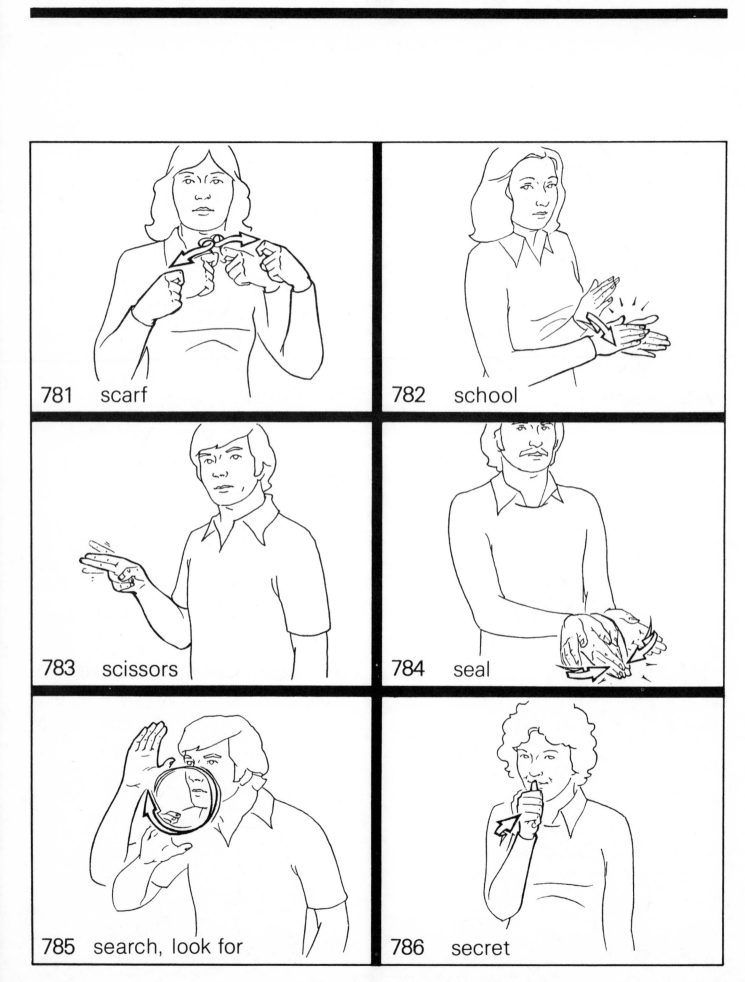

781   scarf

782   school

783   scissors

784   seal

785   search, look for

786   secret

787   see

788   see-saw (AM)

789   sell, store (DM), shop (DM)(N)

790   send, to mail

791   separate, apart

792   several, few, a few

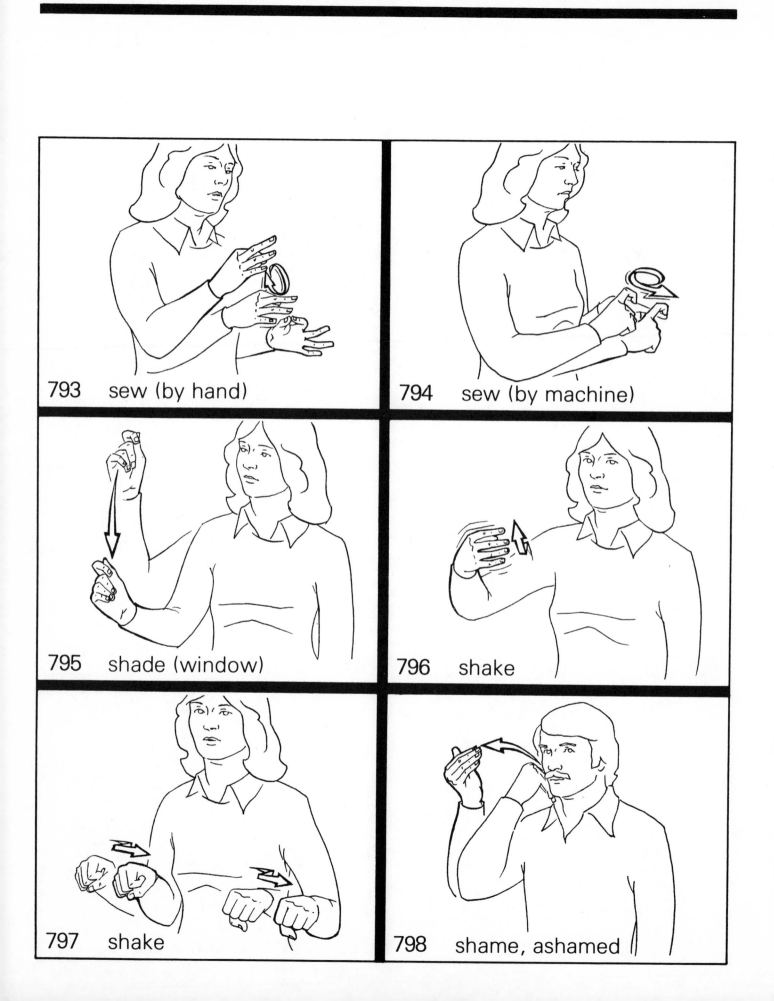

793   sew (by hand)

794   sew (by machine)

795   shade (window)

796   shake

797   shake

798   shame, ashamed

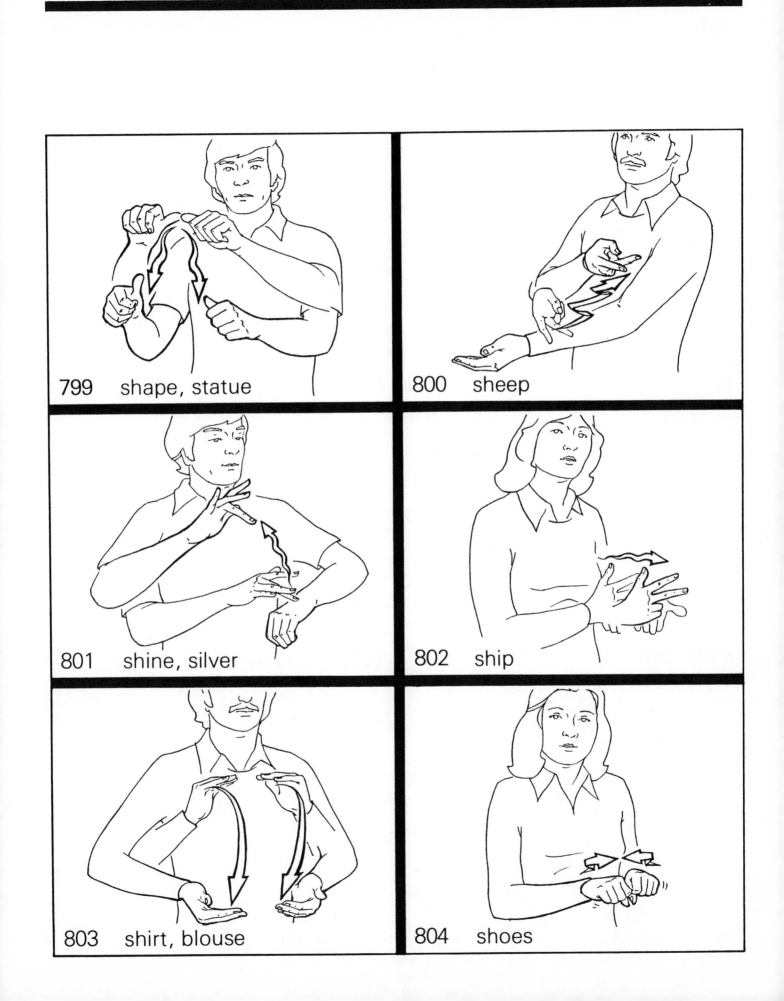

799   shape, statue

800   sheep

801   shine, silver

802   ship

803   shirt, blouse

804   shoes

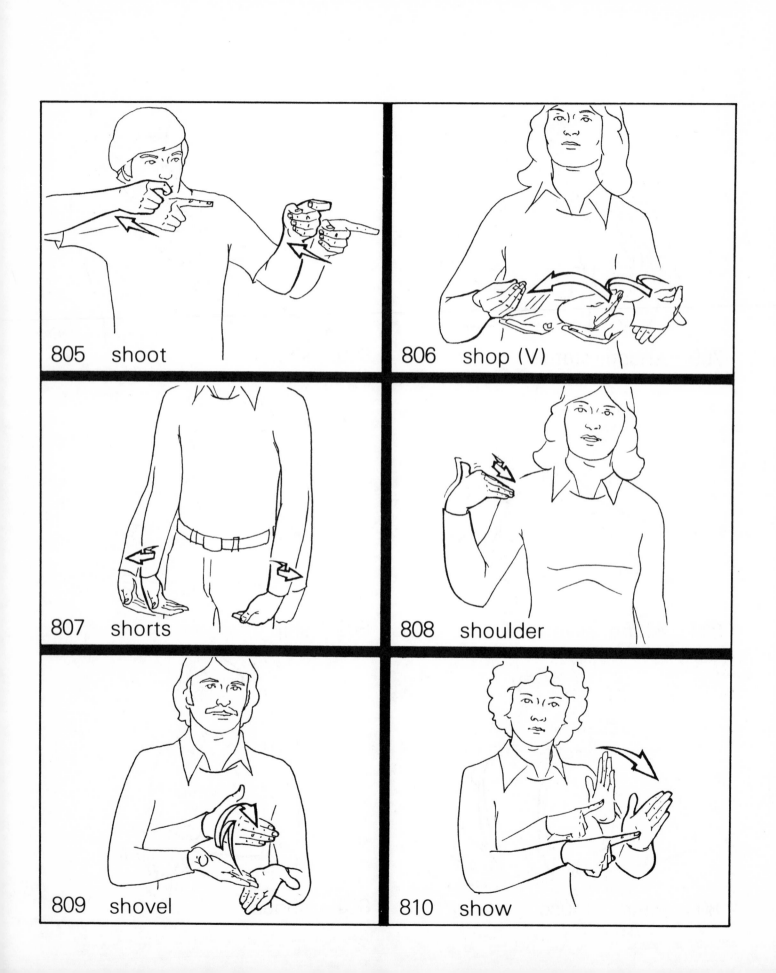

805 shoot

806 shop (V)

807 shorts

808 shoulder

809 shovel

810 show

811 shower

812 shy

813 sick

814 sign (manual)

815 sign, square

816 silly

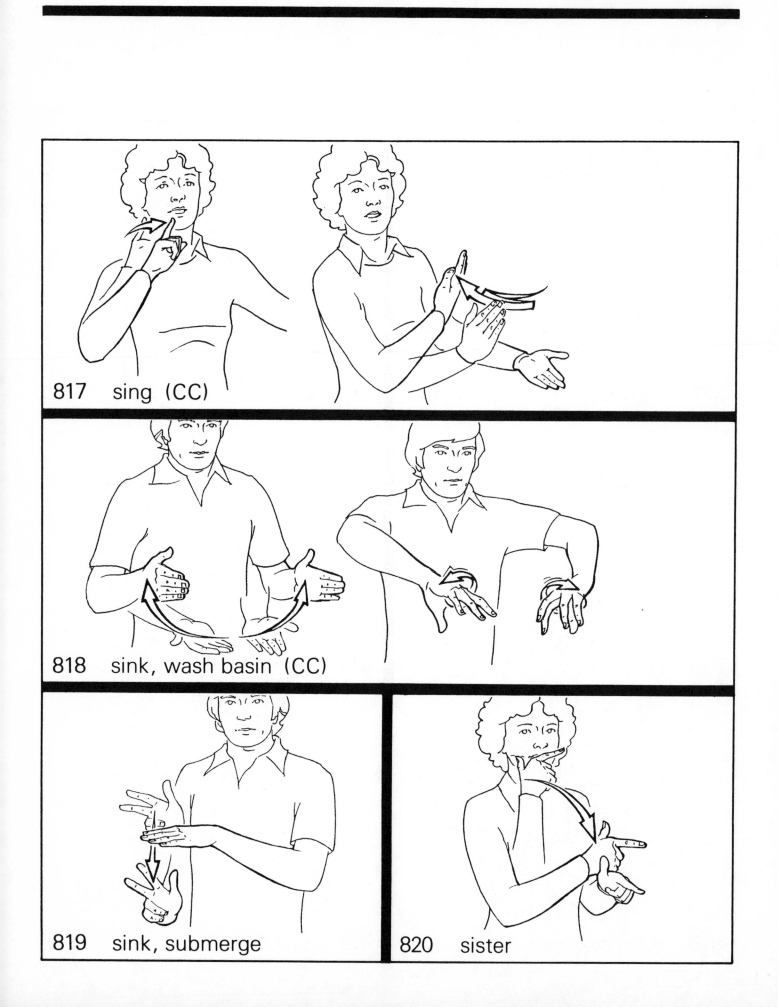

817   sing (CC)

818   sink, wash basin (CC)

819   sink, submerge

820   sister

821   sit, chair (DM)

822   size, what size

823   skate (ice) (AM)

824   skate (roller) (AM)

825   skeleton

826   ski

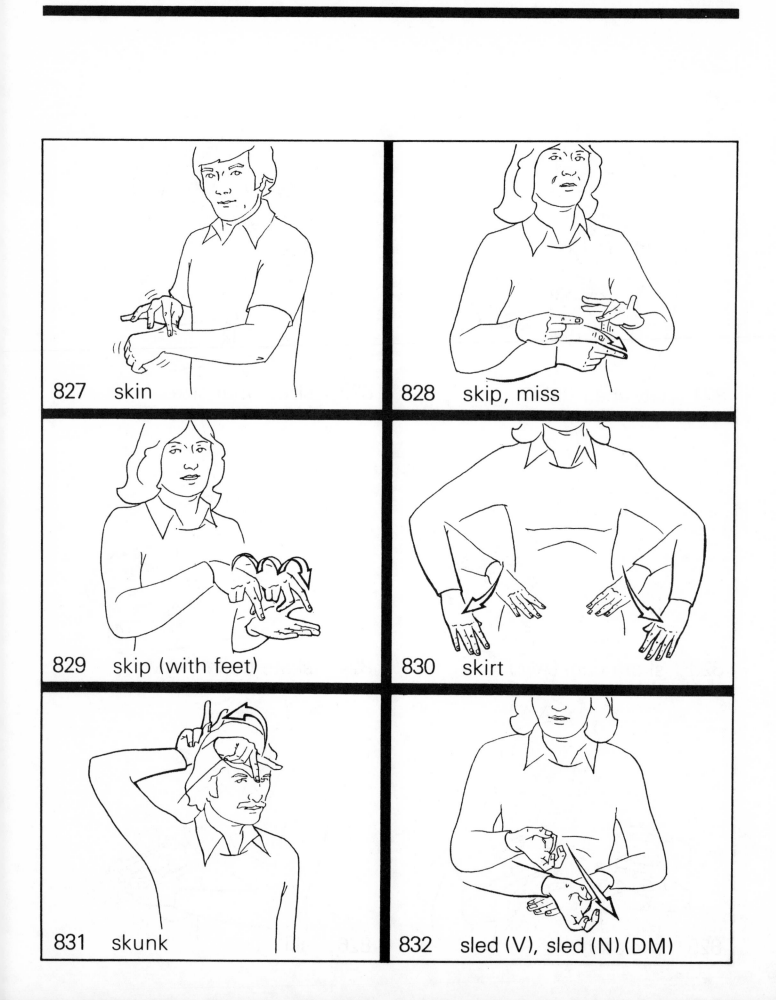

827   skin

828   skip, miss

829   skip (with feet)

830   skirt

831   skunk

832   sled (V), sled (N) (DM)

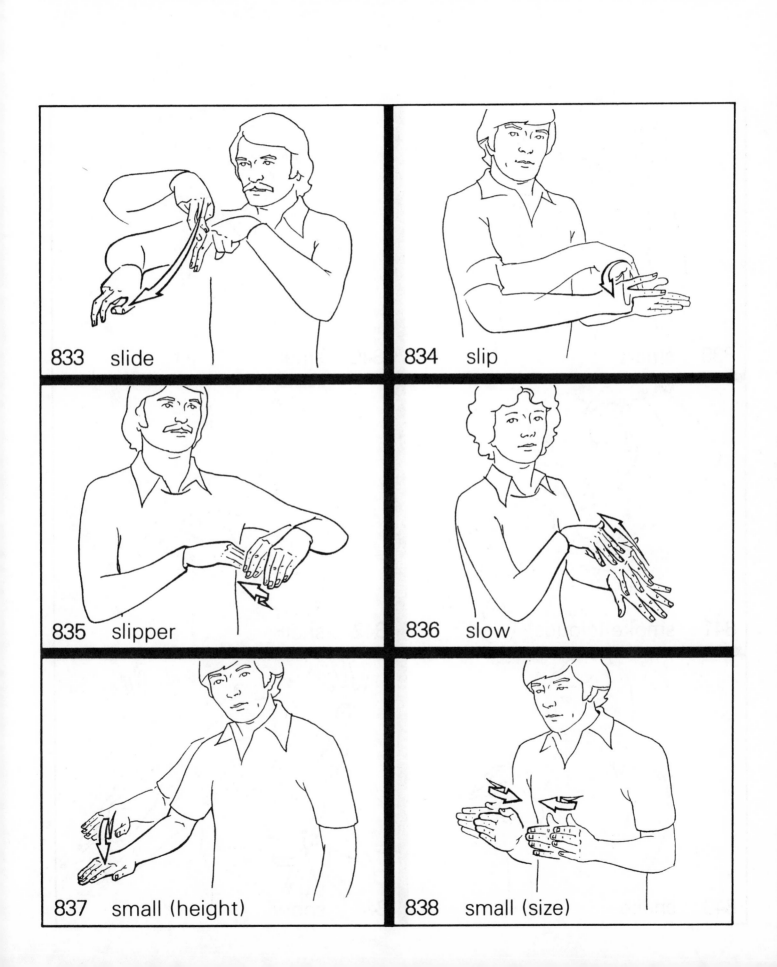

833 slide

834 slip

835 slipper

836 slow

837 small (height)

838 small (size)

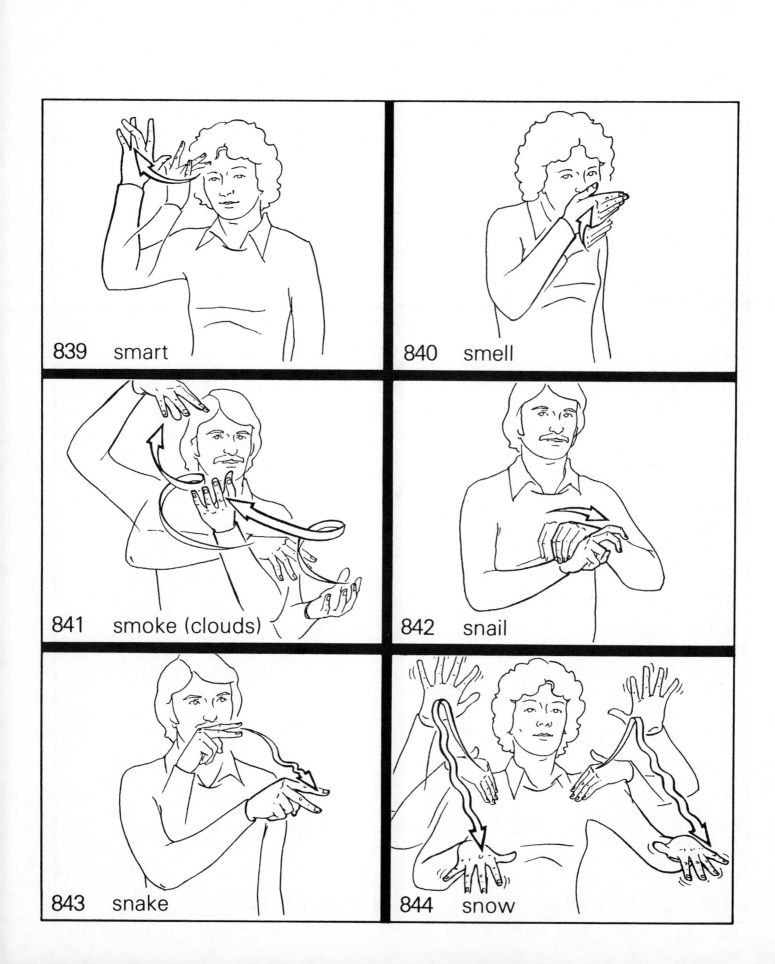

839   smart

840   smell

841   smoke (clouds)

842   snail

843   snake

844   snow

845 sneeze

846 so, well

847 socks (AM)

848 sofa, couch, bench (CC)

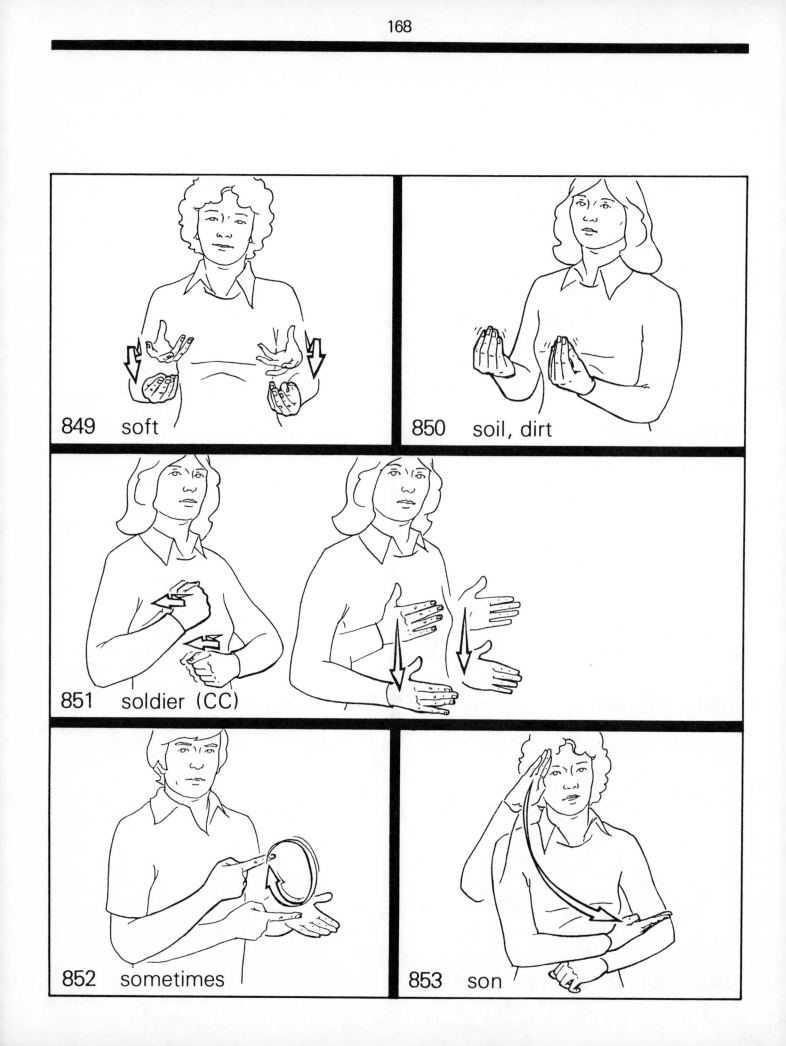

849 soft

850 soil, dirt

851 soldier (CC)

852 sometimes

853 son

854   sorry

855   soup

856   South

857   spaghetti

858   space (outer-)

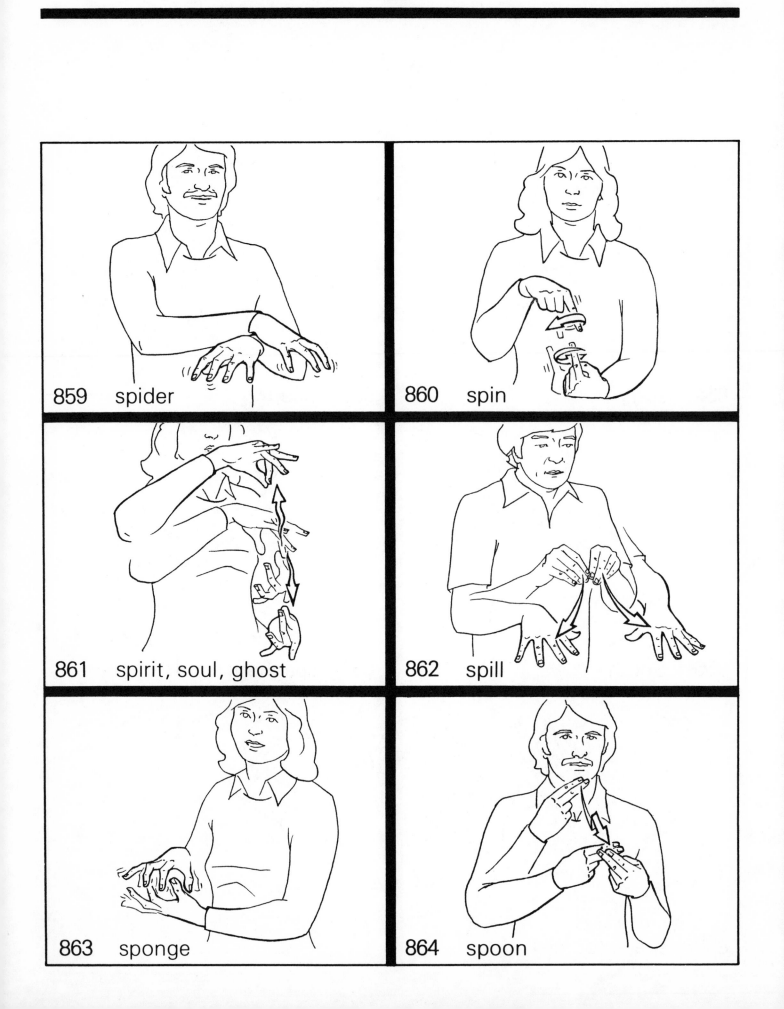

859 spider

860 spin

861 spirit, soul, ghost

862 spill

863 sponge

864 spoon

865 sprinkler (CC)

866 squirrel, chipmunk

867 stairway

868 stamp

869 stand

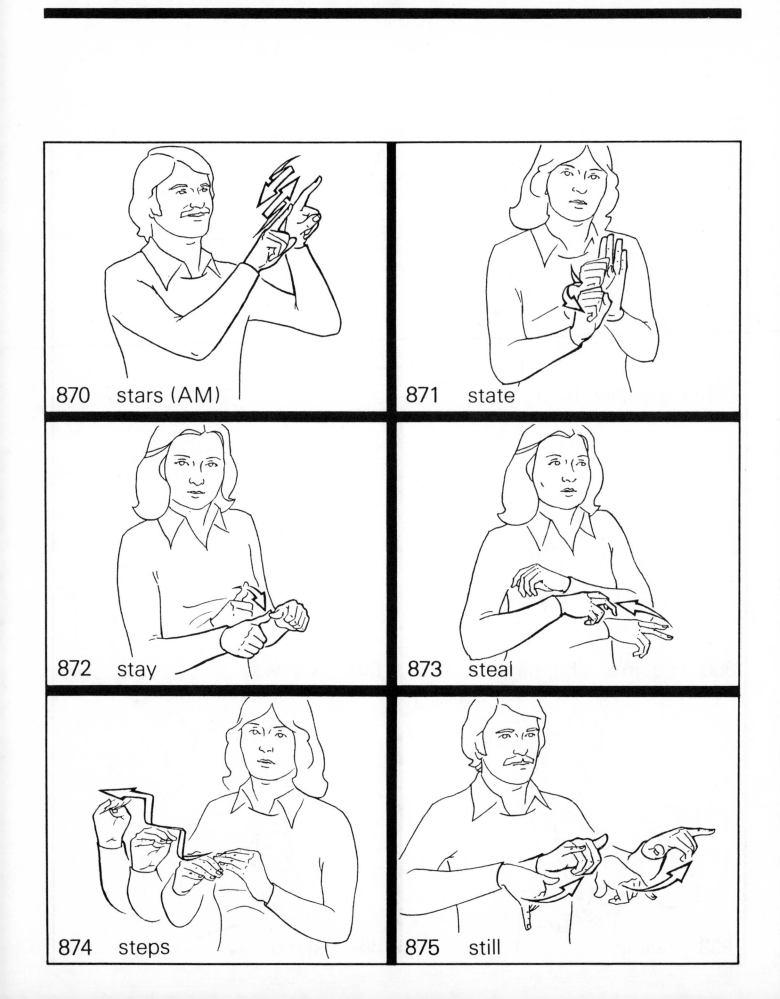

870   stars (AM)

871   state

872   stay

873   steal

874   steps

875   still

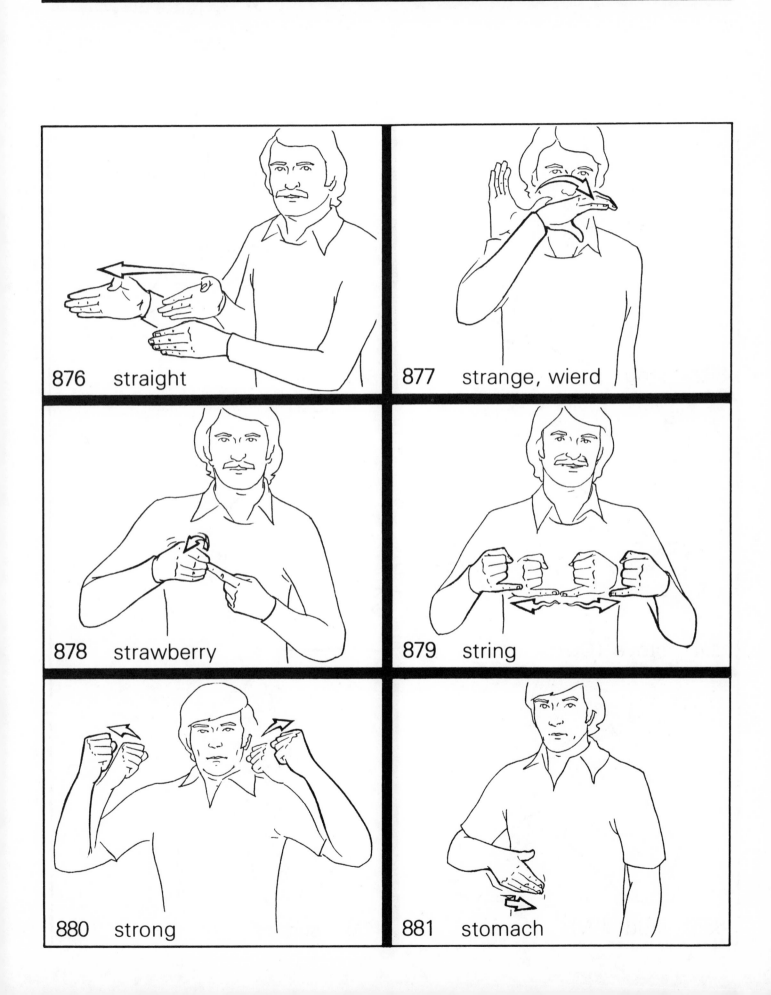

876 straight

877 strange, wierd

878 strawberry

879 string

880 strong

881 stomach

882   stop

883   story

884   stove (CC)

885   study (W)

886   sugar

887   submarine (CC)

888   suffer

889   suitcase, briefcase, purse

890   summer

891   sun

892   sunshine (CC)

893   suppose, imagine

894   surprise

895   sweater, pull over (V)

896   sweep

897   sweet, dear

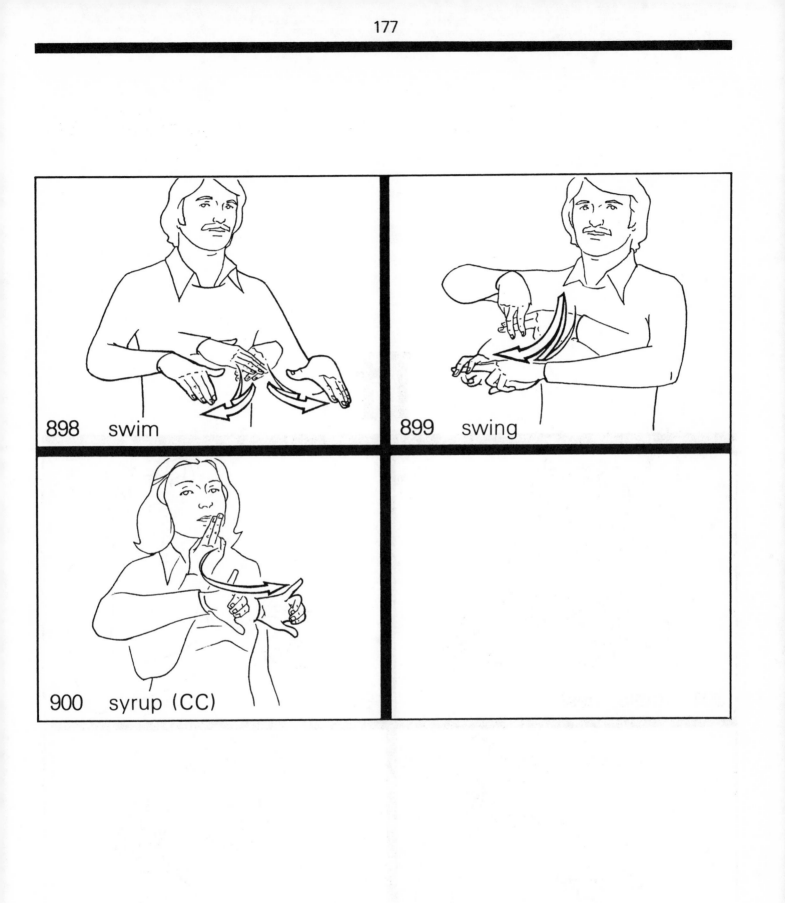

898   swim

899   swing

900   syrup (CC)

Tt

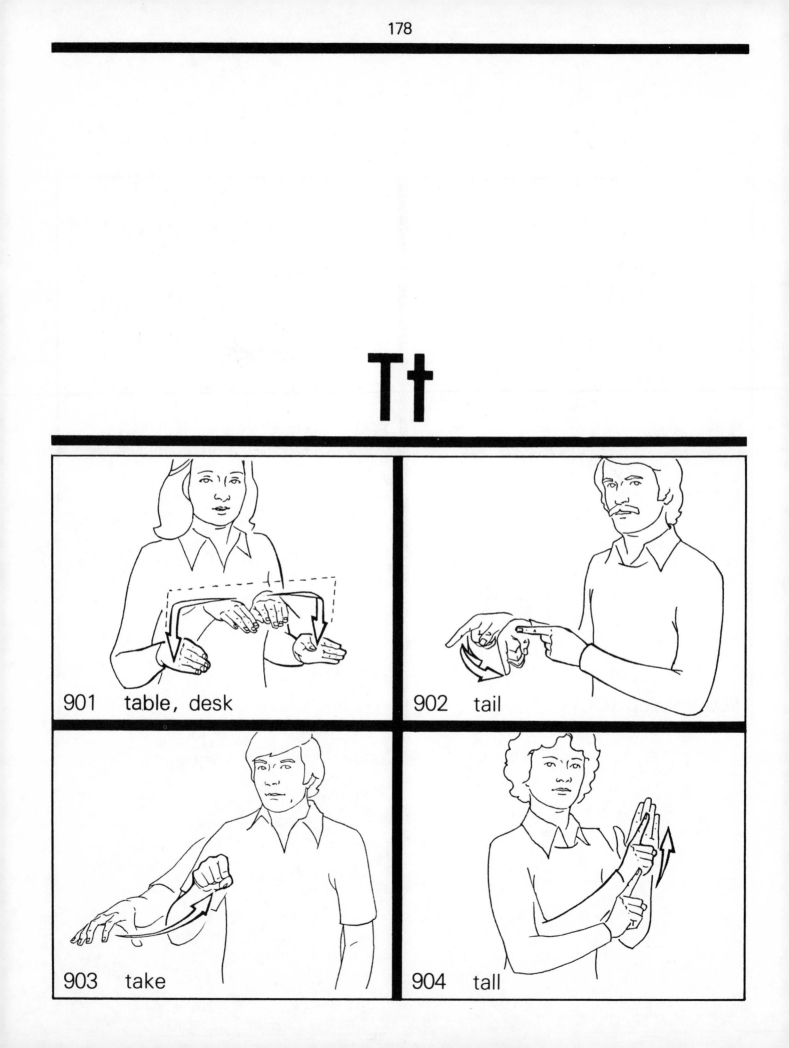

901 table, desk

902 tail

903 take

904 tall

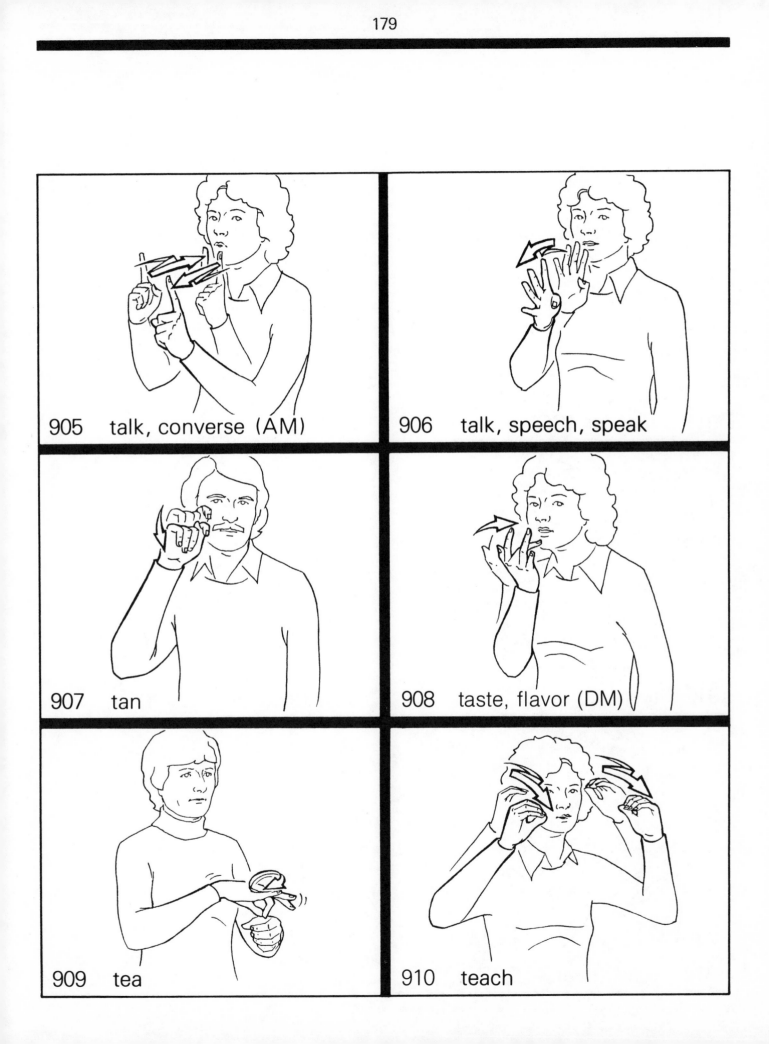

905   talk, converse (AM)

906   talk, speech, speak

907   tan

908   taste, flavor (DM)

909   tea

910   teach

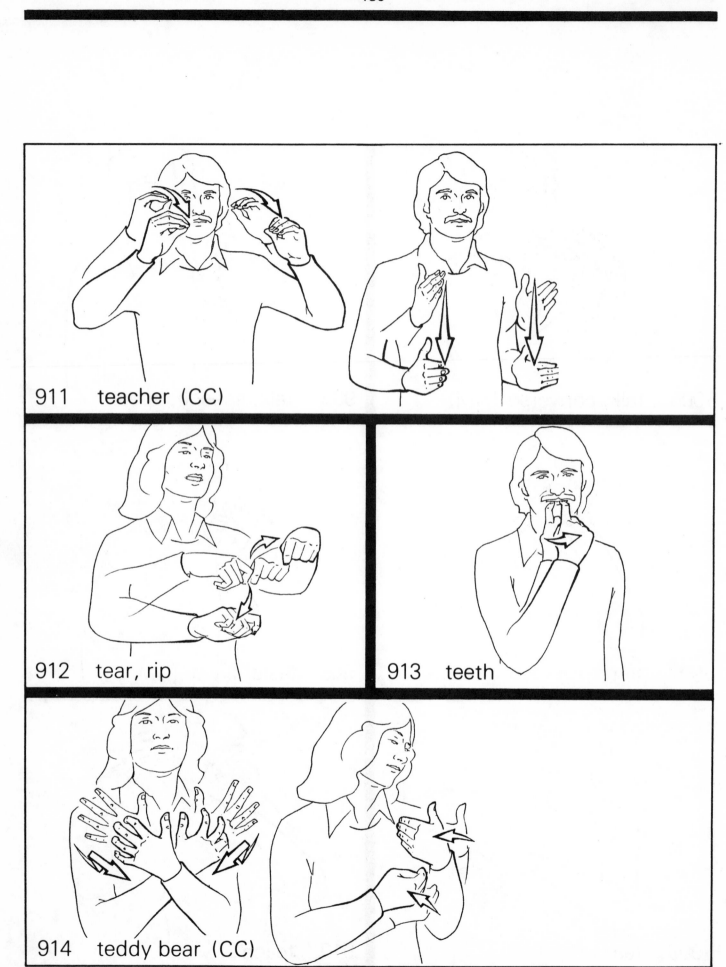

911   teacher (CC)

912   tear, rip

913   teeth

914   teddy bear (CC)

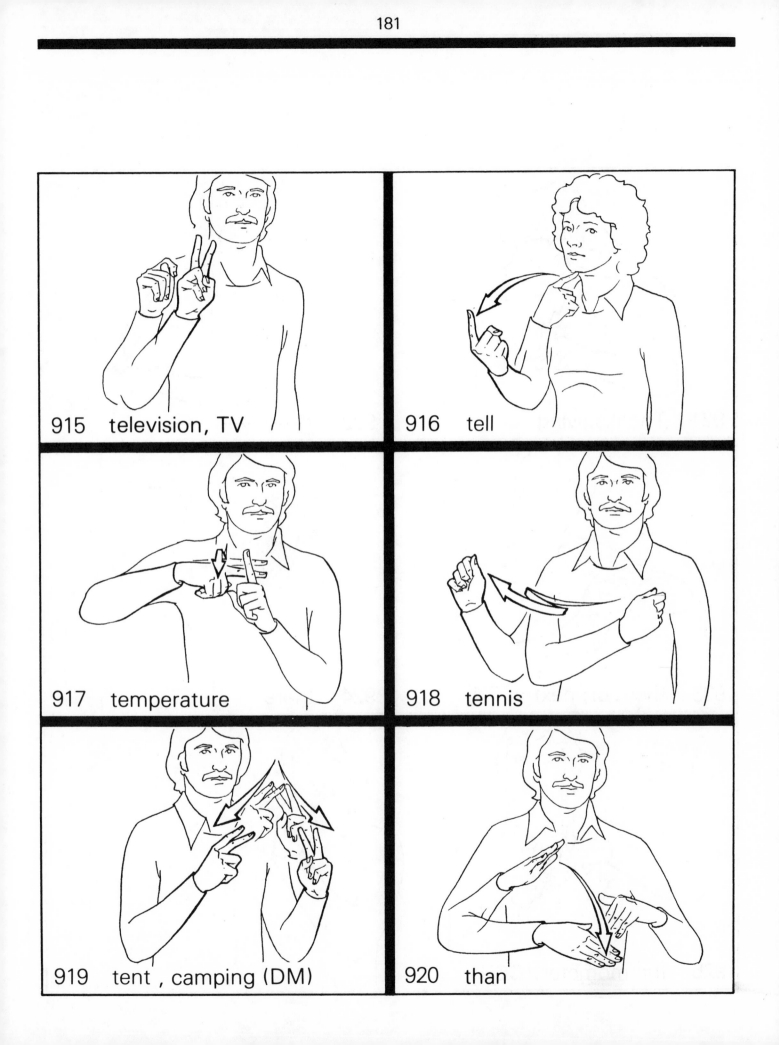

915　television, TV

916　tell

917　temperature

918　tennis

919　tent , camping (DM)

920　than

921   Thanksgiving

922   thank you

923   then, or, next

924   there

925   thermometer (CC)

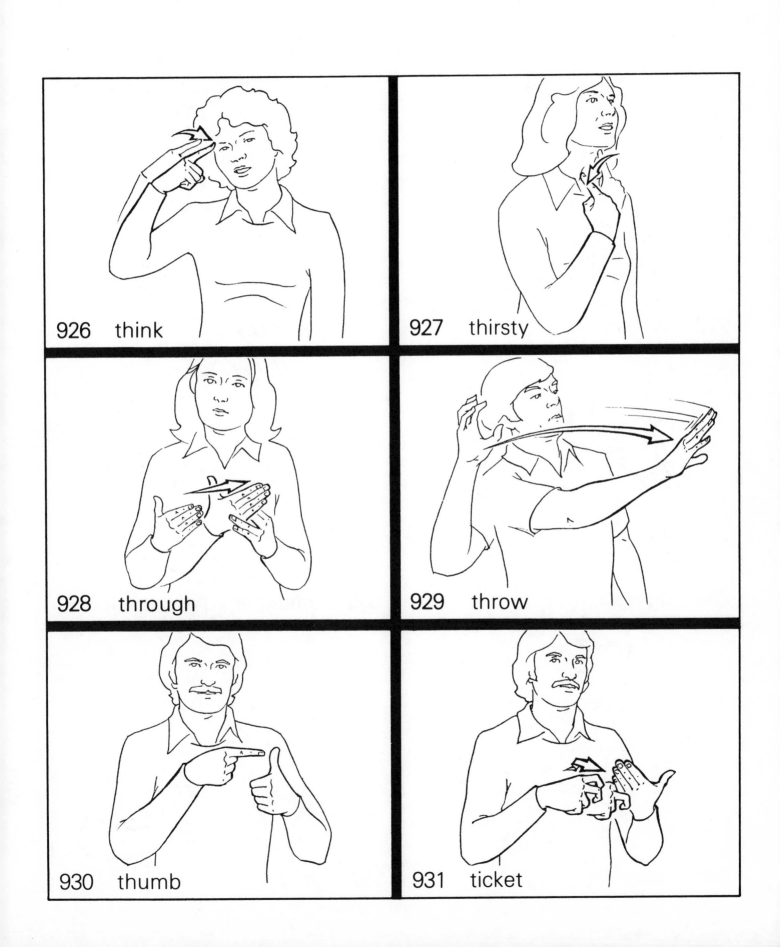

926 think

927 thirsty

928 through

929 throw

930 thumb

931 ticket

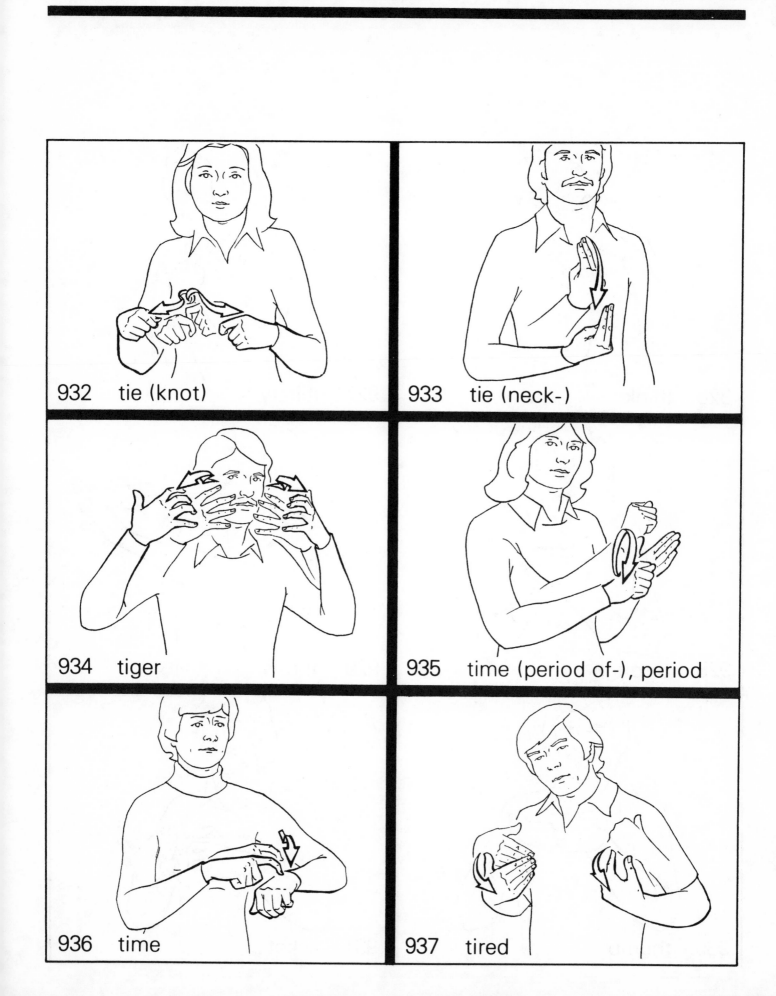

932   tie (knot)

933   tie (neck-)

934   tiger

935   time (period of-), period

936   time

937   tired

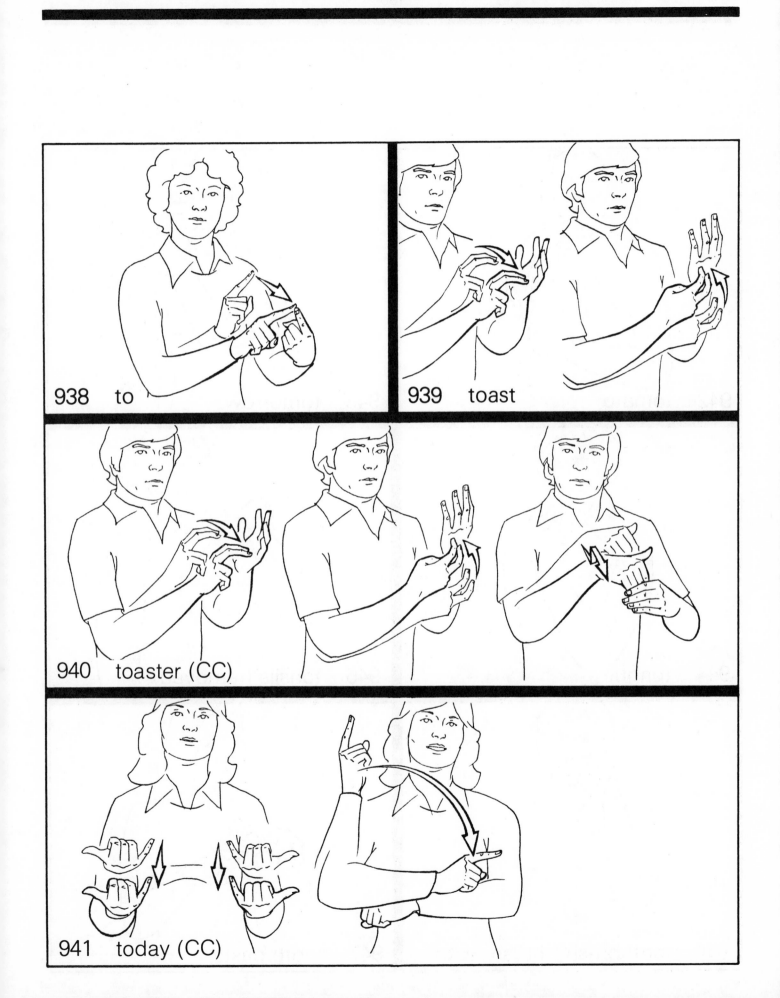

938   to

939   toast

940   toaster (CC)

941   today (CC)

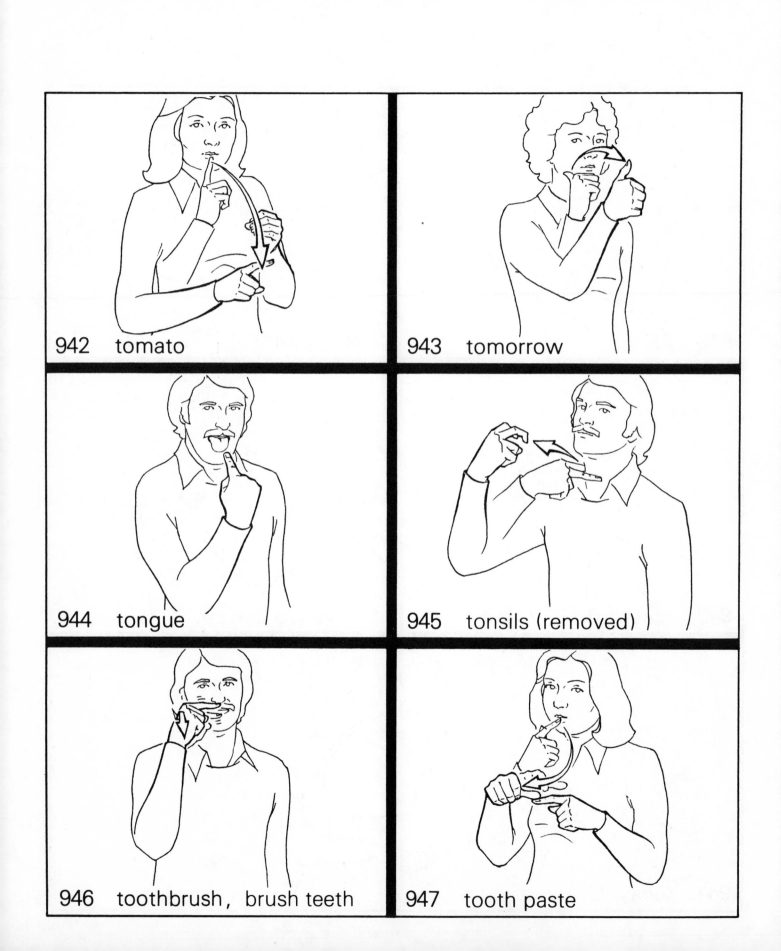

942 tomato

943 tomorrow

944 tongue

945 tonsils (removed)

946 toothbrush, brush teeth

947 tooth paste

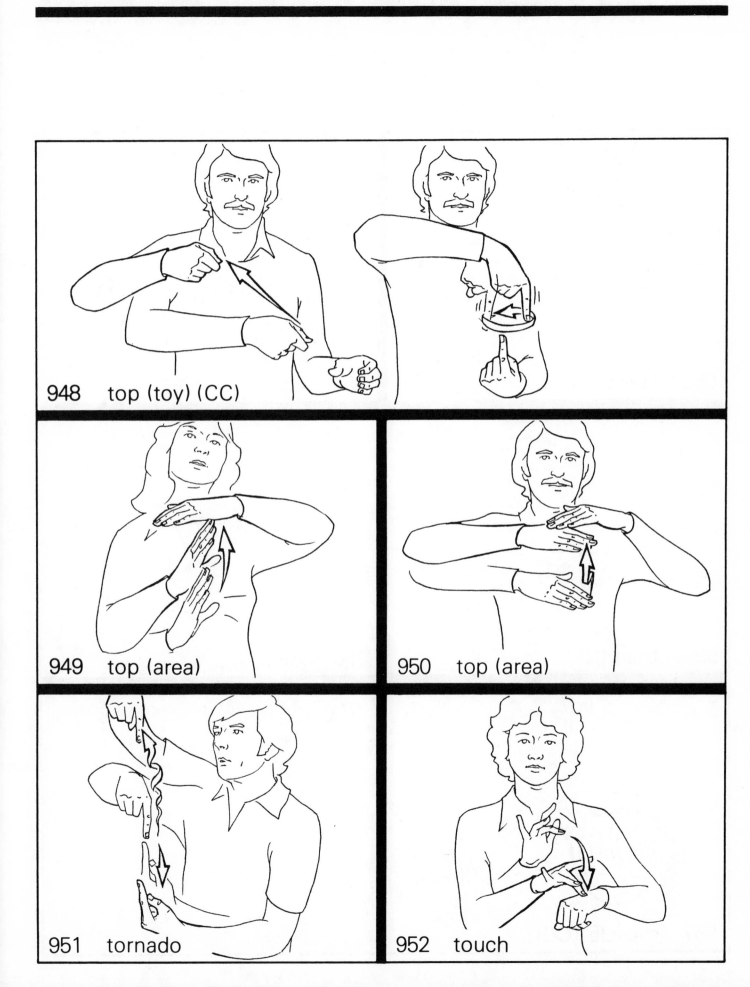

948 top (toy) (CC)

949 top (area)

950 top (area)

951 tornado

952 touch

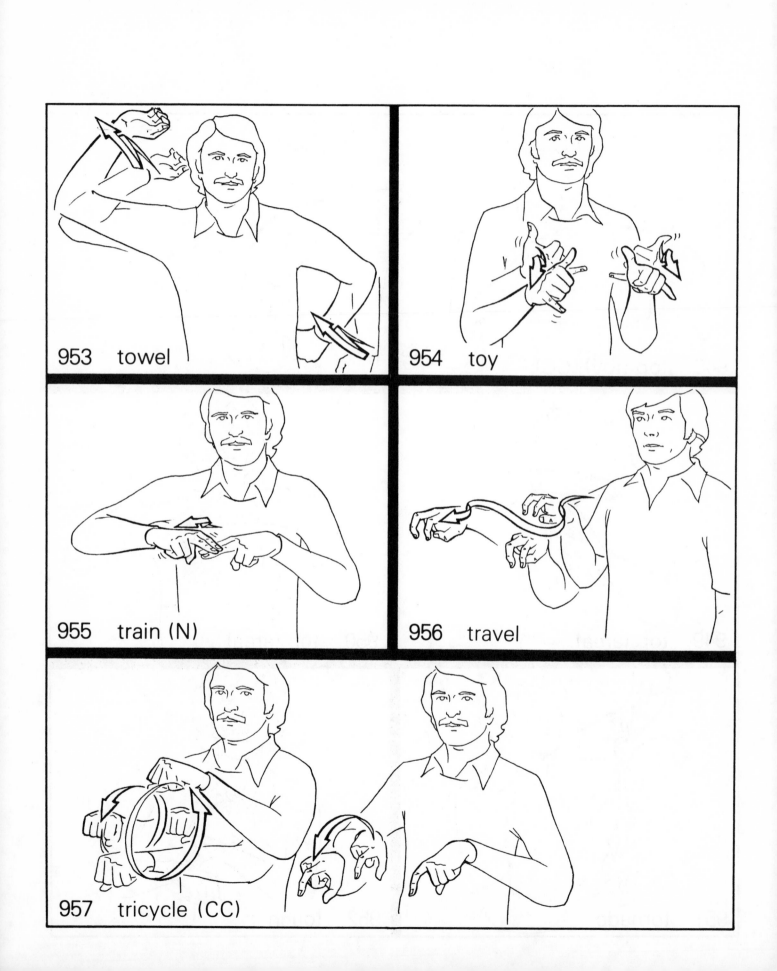

953 towel

954 toy

955 train (N)

956 travel

957 tricycle (CC)

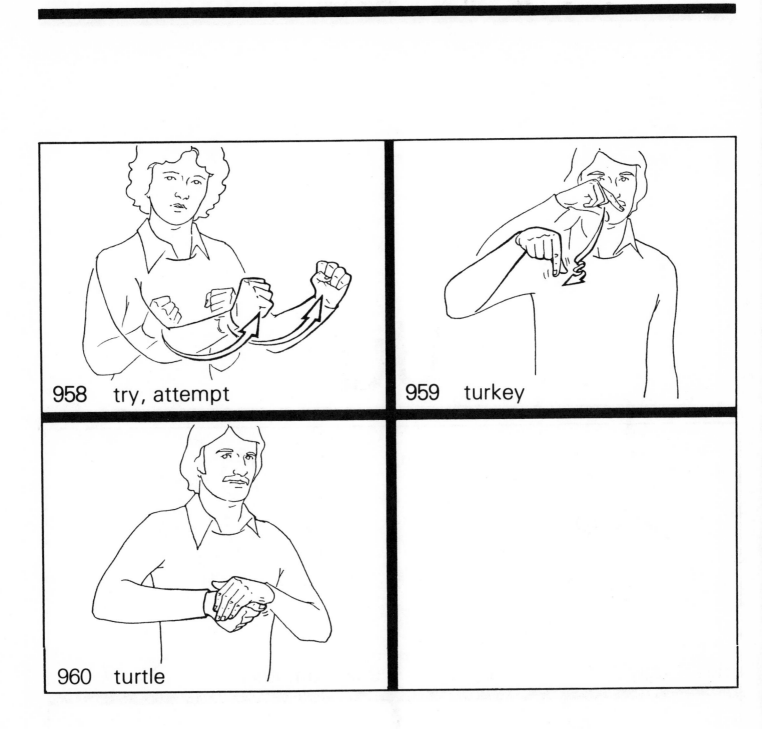

958   try, attempt

959   turkey

960   turtle

Uu

961   ugly

962   umbrella

963   uncle

964   understand

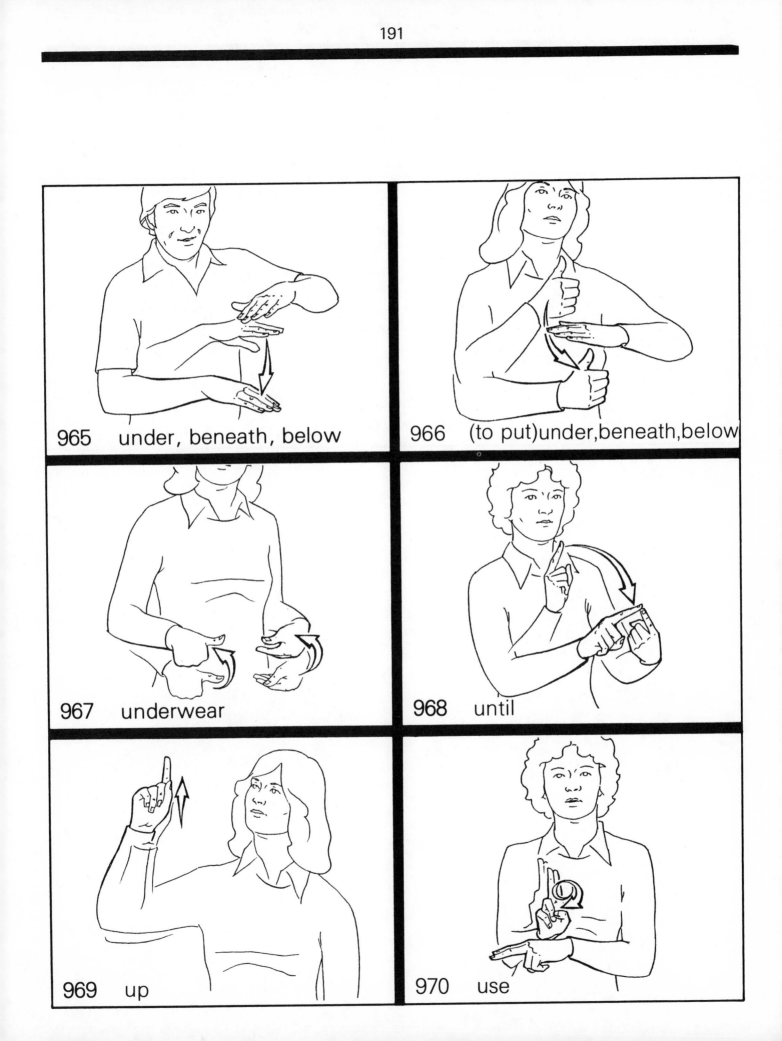

965 under, beneath, below

966 (to put)under,beneath,below

967 underwear

968 until

969 up

970 use

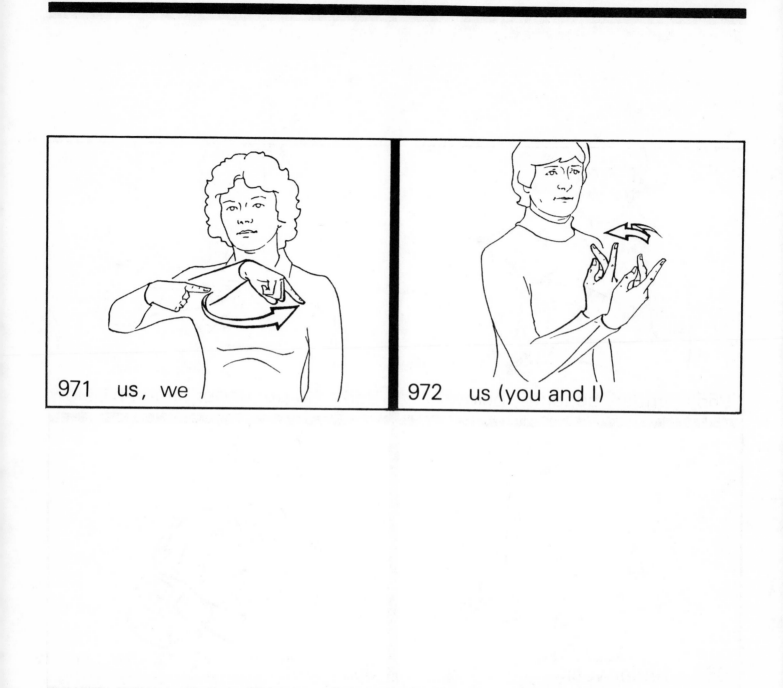

971 us, we

972 us (you and I)

Vv

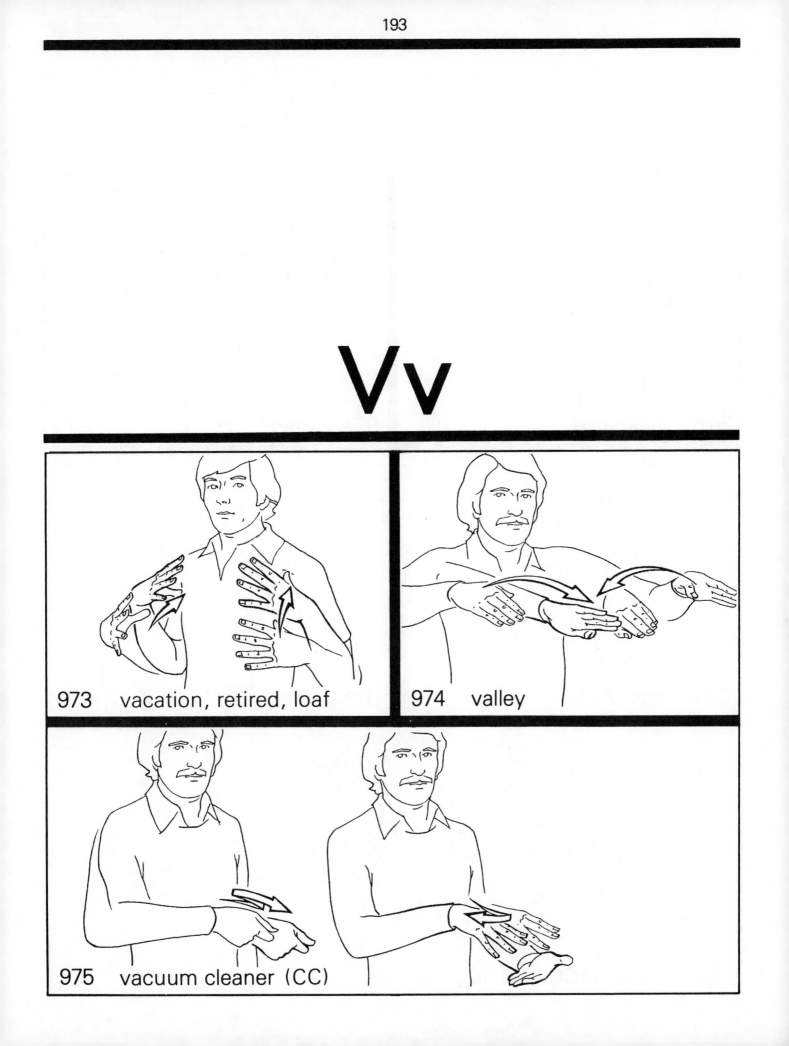

973 vacation, retired, loaf

974 valley

975 vacuum cleaner (CC)

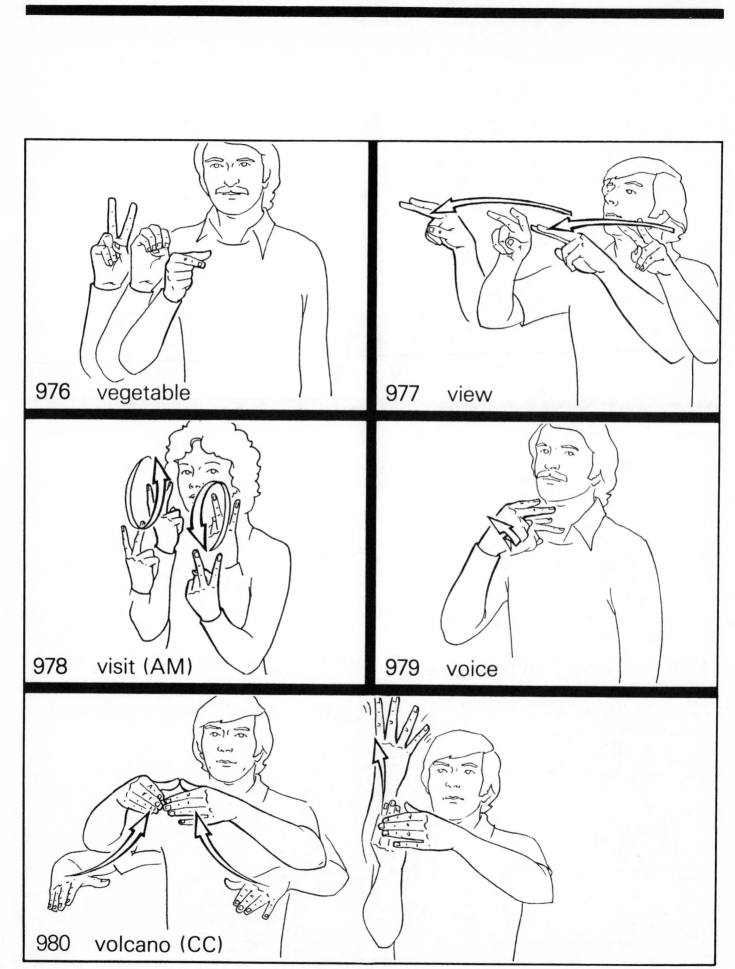

976　vegetable

977　view

978　visit (AM)

979　voice

980　volcano (CC)

Ww

981   wagon (station-)

982   wagon (toy)

983   wait (W)

984   wake-up

985   waitress (CC)

986   wall

987   want

988   war, battle

989   warm

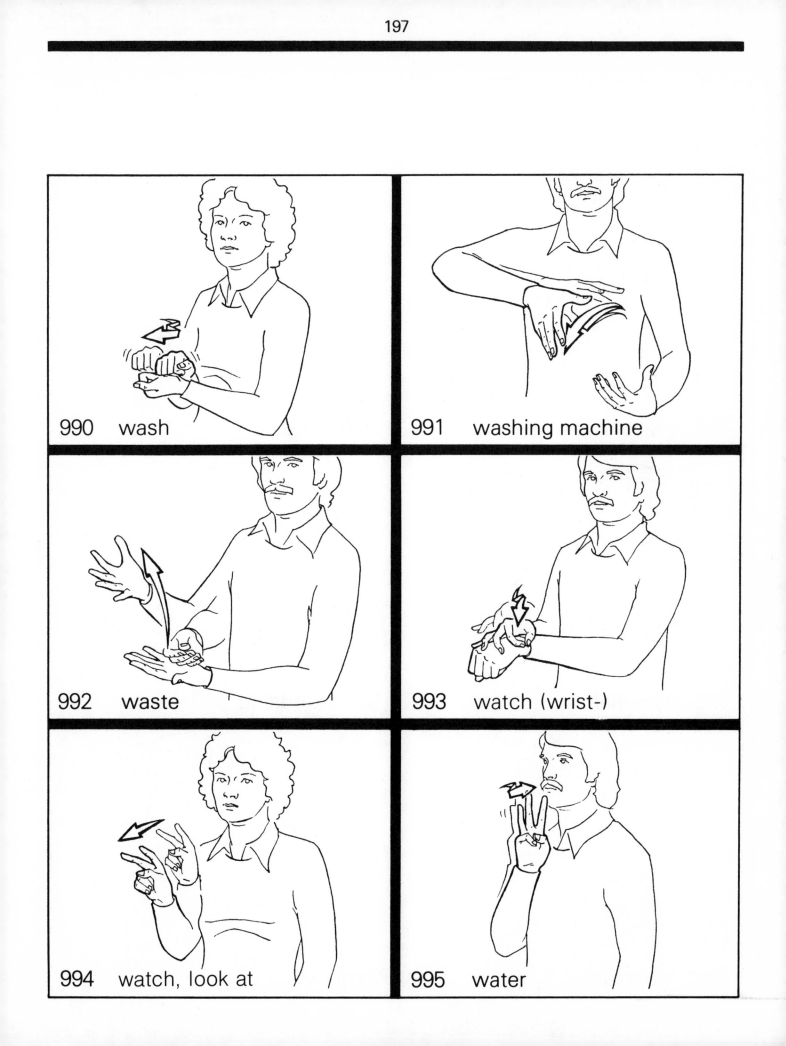

990 wash

991 washing machine

992 waste

993 watch (wrist-)

994 watch, look at

995 water

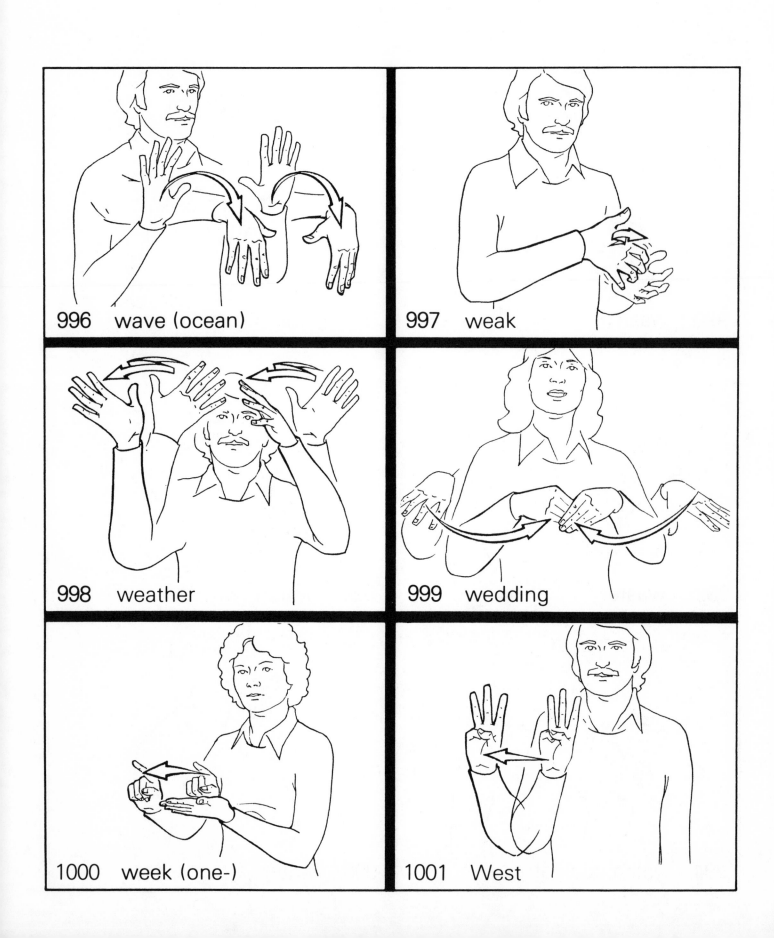

996   wave (ocean)

997   weak

998   weather

999   wedding

1000   week (one-)

1001   West

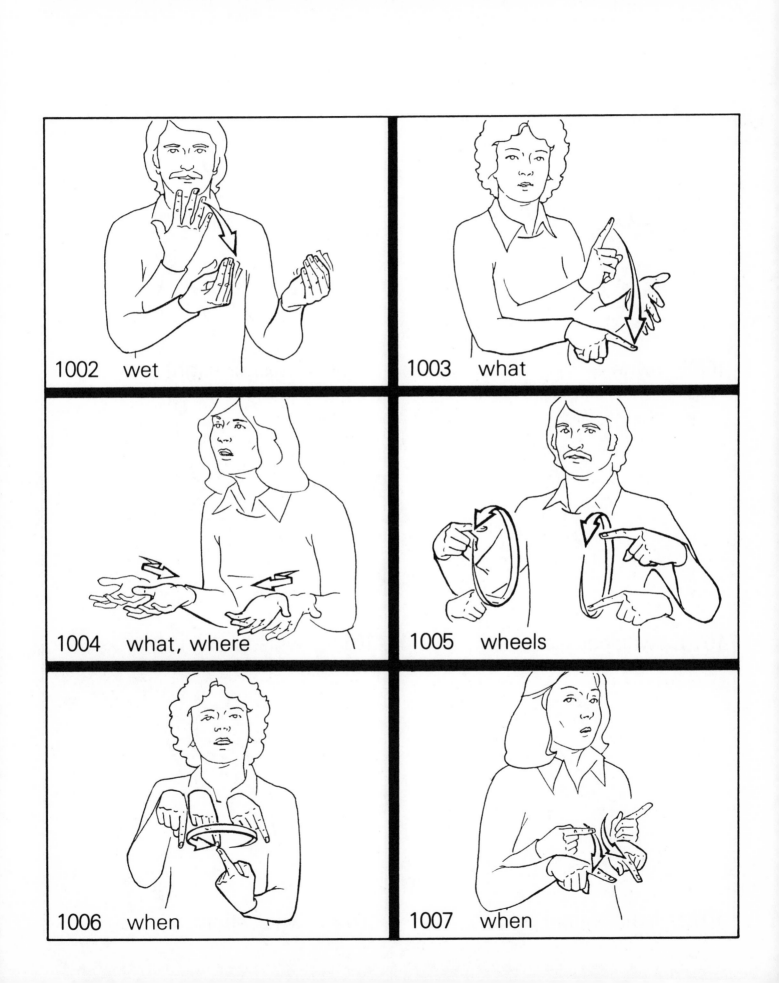

1002   wet

1003   what

1004   what, where

1005   wheels

1006   when

1007   when

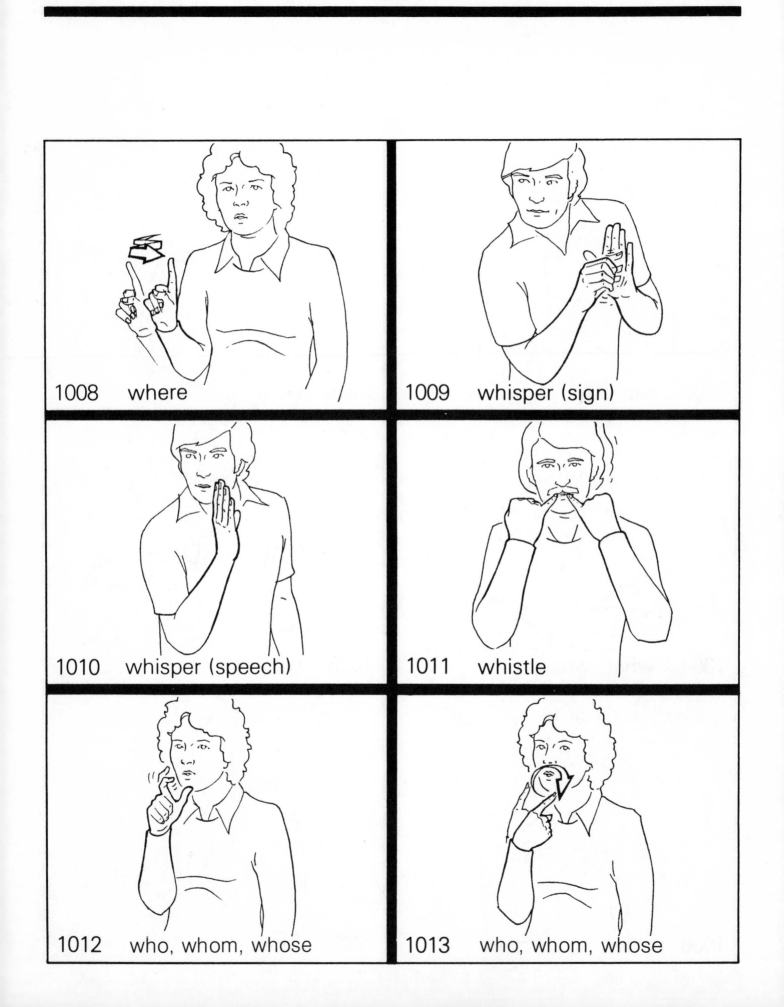

1008   where

1009   whisper (sign)

1010   whisper (speech)

1011   whistle

1012   who, whom, whose

1013   who, whom, whose

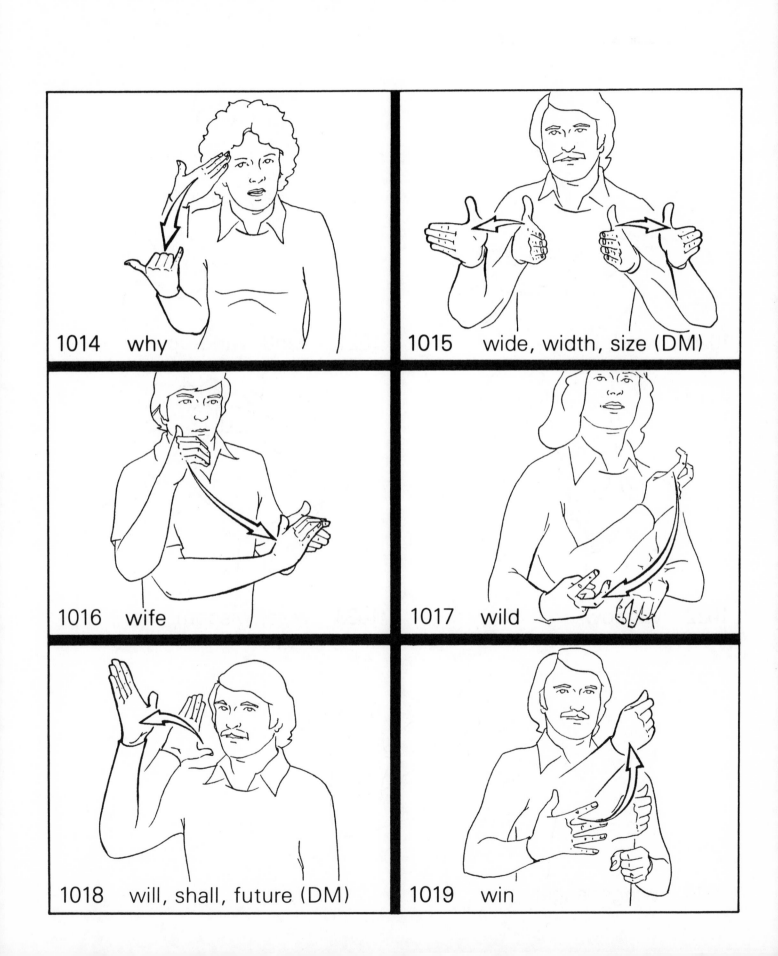

1014　why

1015　wide, width, size (DM)

1016　wife

1017　wild

1018　will, shall, future (DM)

1019　win

1020   wind, breeze

1021   wind, wind-up

1022   window

1023   wise, wisdom

1024   wings, angel

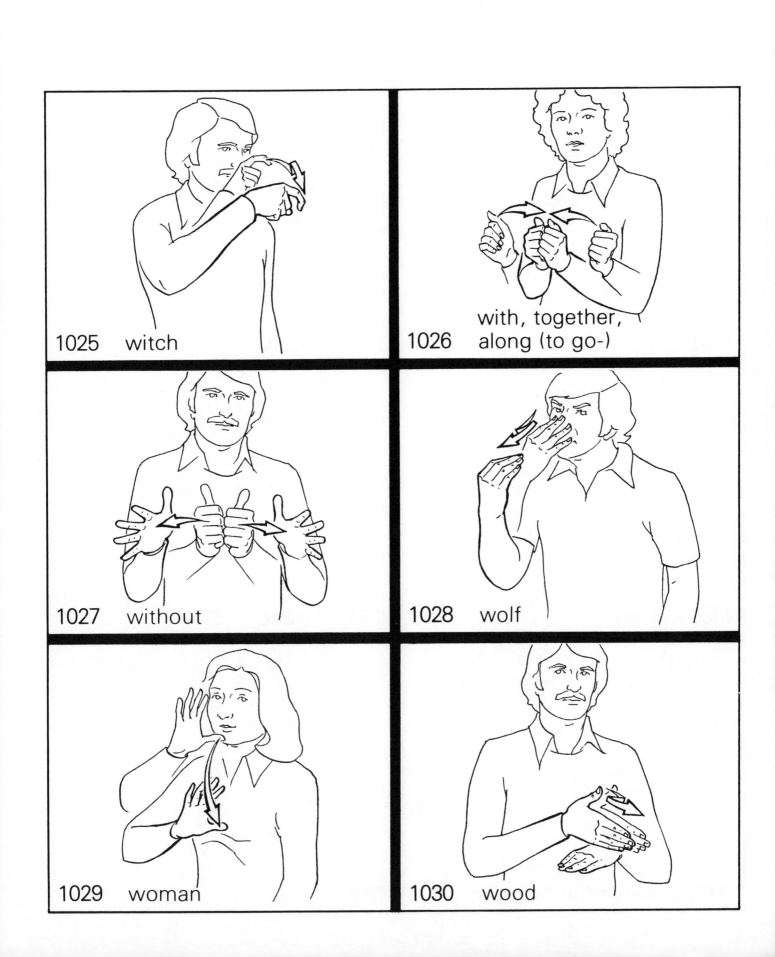

1025 witch

1026 with, together, along (to go-)

1027 without

1028 wolf

1029 woman

1030 wood

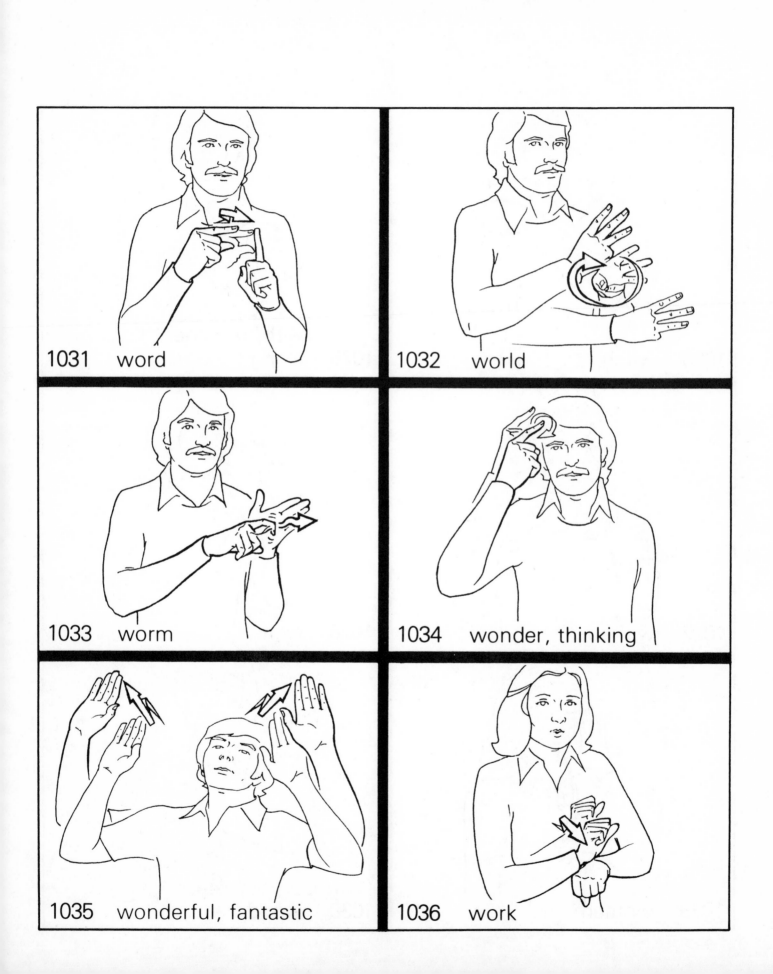

1031   word

1032   world

1033   worm

1034   wonder, thinking

1035   wonderful, fantastic

1036   work

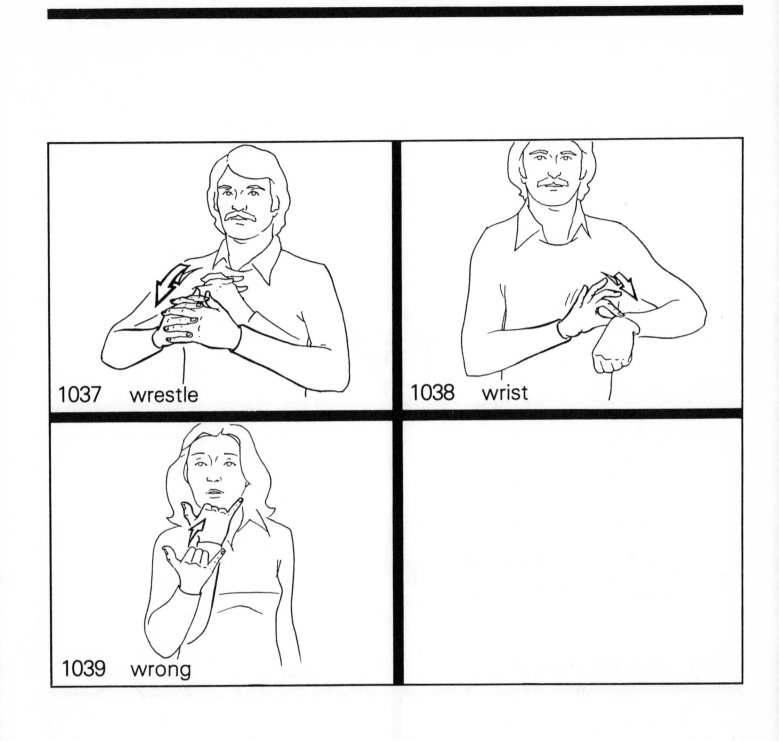

1037   wrestle

1038   wrist

1039   wrong

Yy

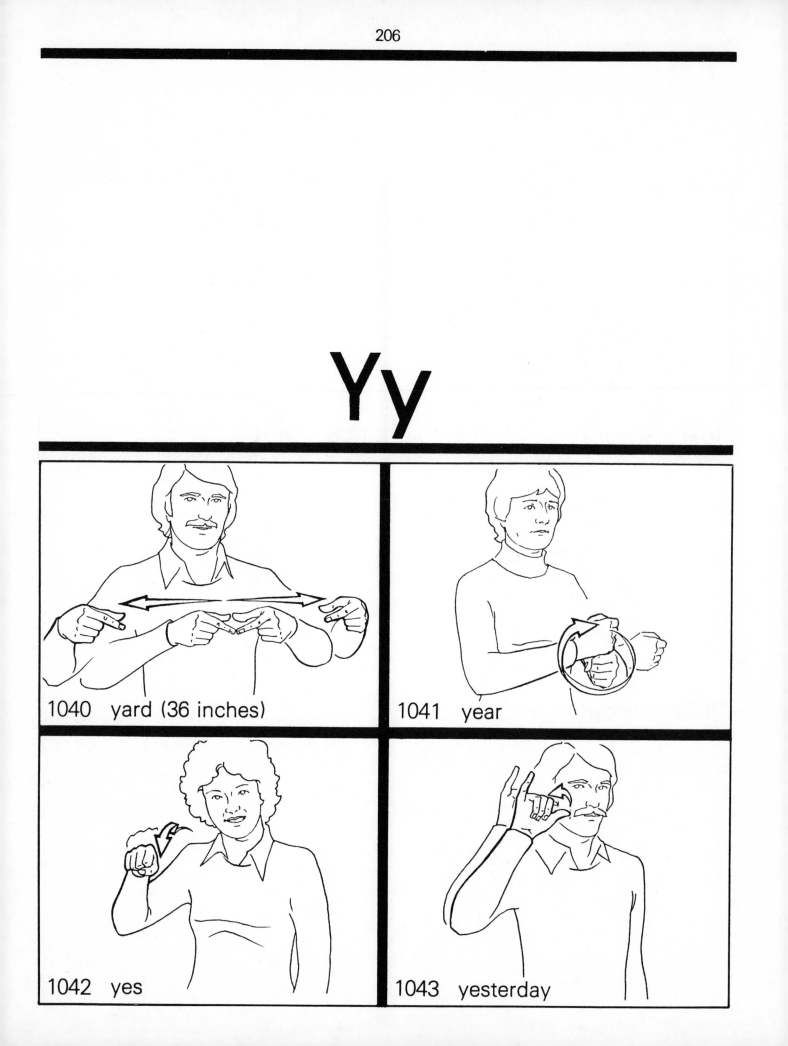

1040 yard (36 inches)

1041 year

1042 yes

1043 yesterday

1044   you

1045   young, youth

1046   your

1047   yourself

1048   yo-yo

Zz

1049   zebra (CC)

1050   zip up, zipper (DM)

NUMBERS
american sign language

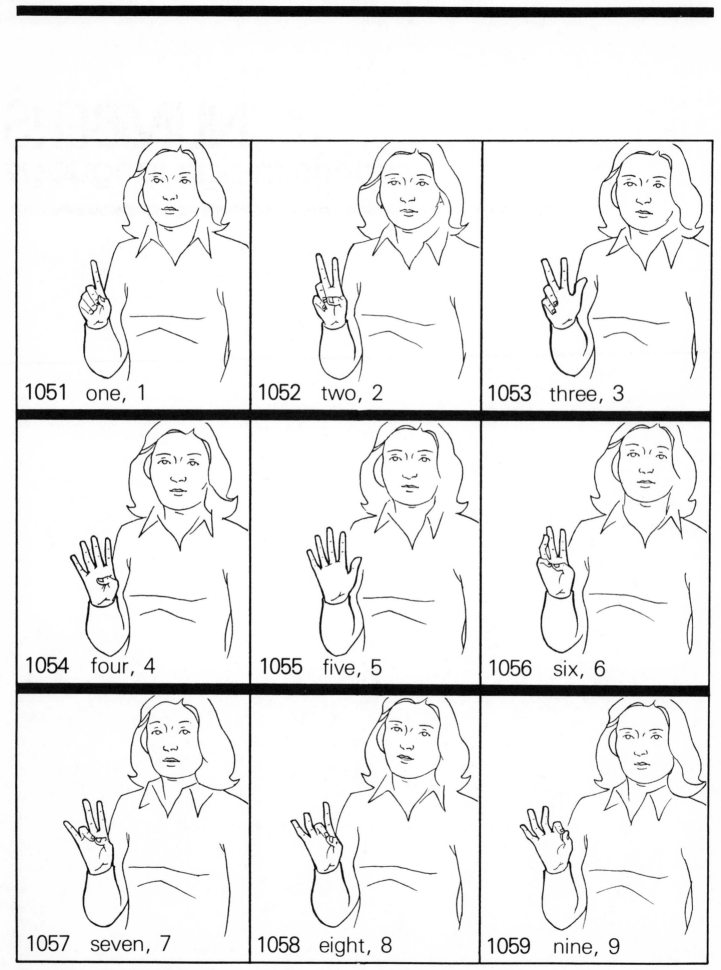

1051   one, 1

1052   two, 2

1053   three, 3

1054   four, 4

1055   five, 5

1056   six, 6

1057   seven, 7

1058   eight, 8

1059   nine, 9

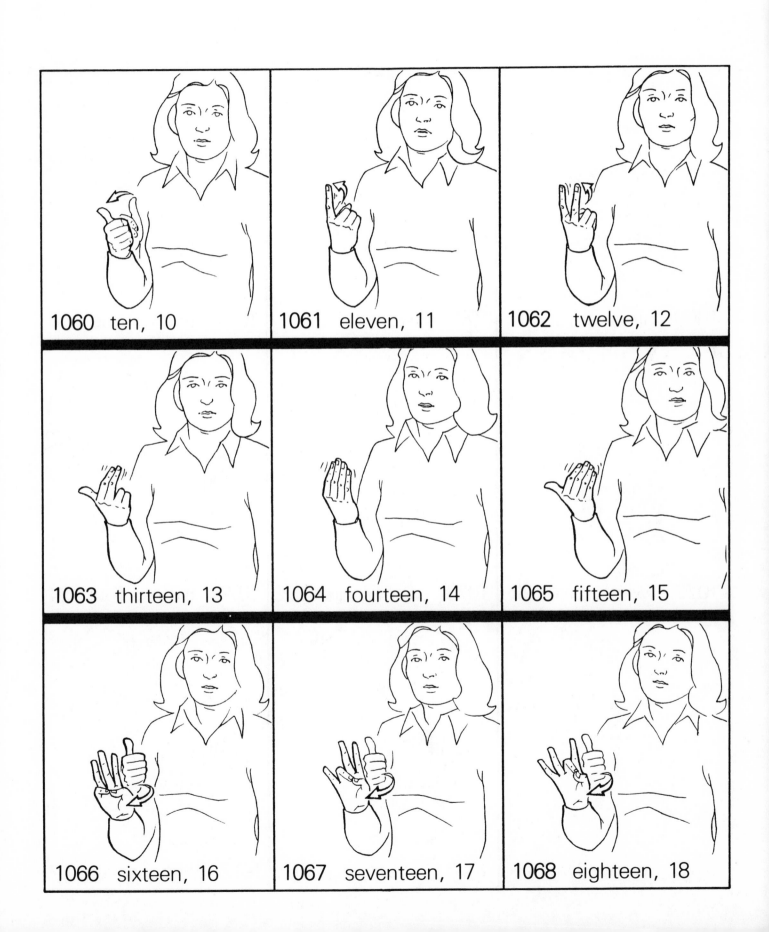

1060 ten, 10

1061 eleven, 11

1062 twelve, 12

1063 thirteen, 13

1064 fourteen, 14

1065 fifteen, 15

1066 sixteen, 16

1067 seventeen, 17

1068 eighteen, 18

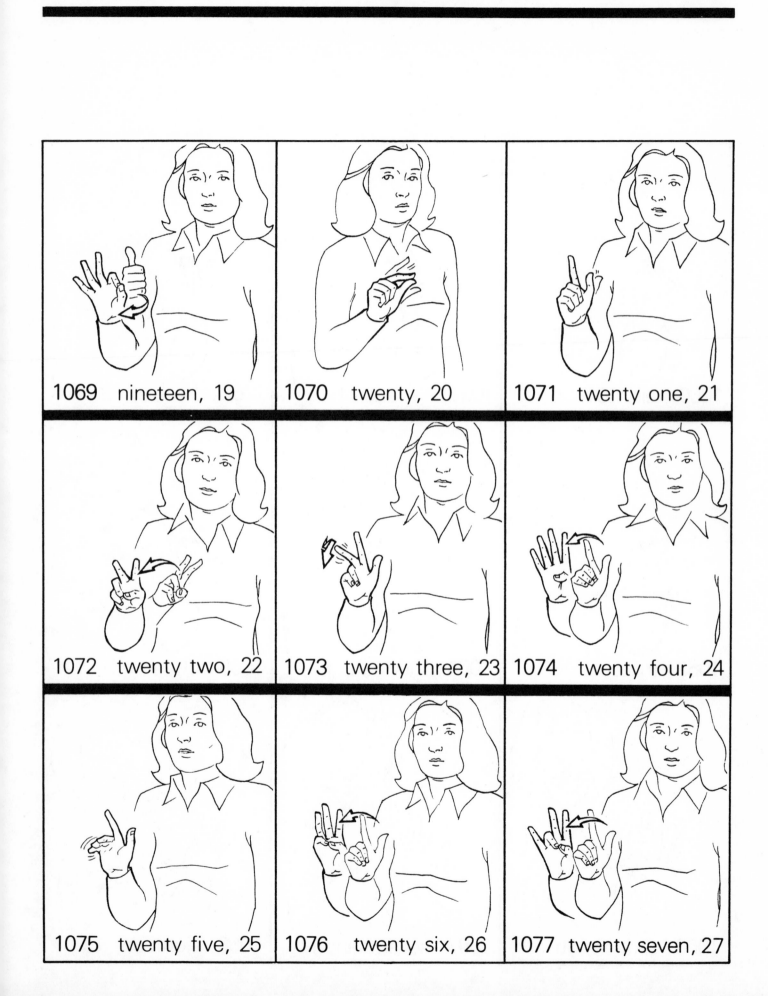

1069   nineteen, 19

1070   twenty, 20

1071   twenty one, 21

1072   twenty two, 22

1073   twenty three, 23

1074   twenty four, 24

1075   twenty five, 25

1076   twenty six, 26

1077   twenty seven, 27

1078 twenty eight, 28

1079 twenty nine, 29

1080 thirty, 30

1081 zero, 0

1082 hundred, 100

1083 thousand, 1,000

1084 million, 1,000,000

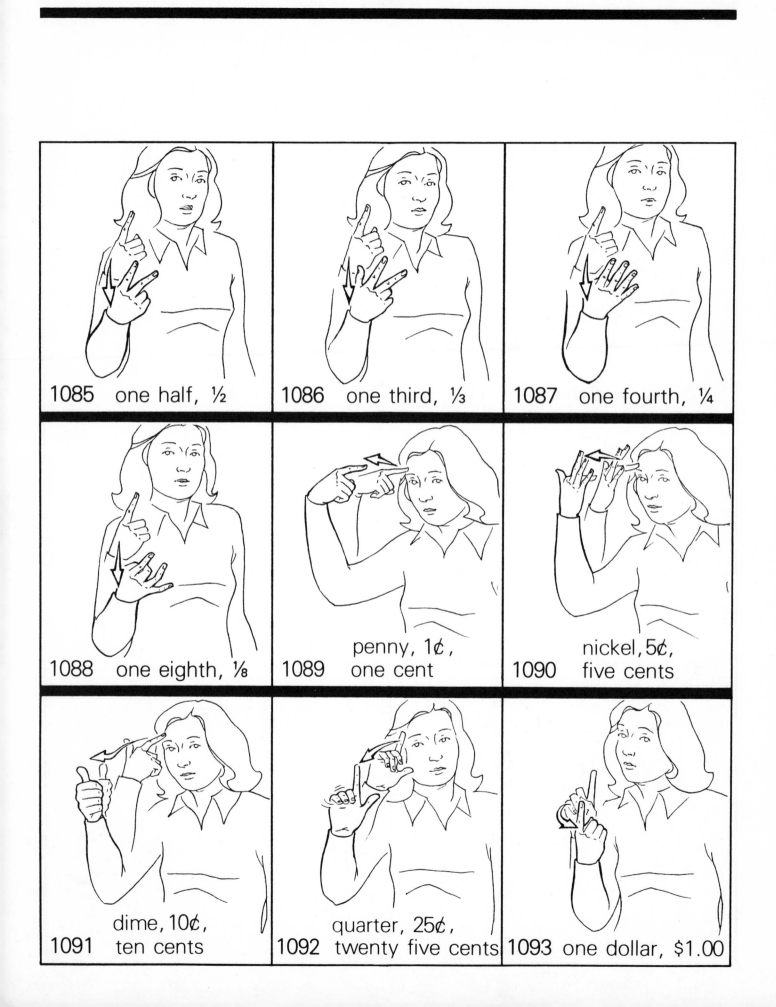

1085 one half, ½

1086 one third, ⅓

1087 one fourth, ¼

1088 one eighth, ⅛

1089 penny, 1¢,
one cent

1090 nickel, 5¢,
five cents

1091 dime, 10¢,
ten cents

1092 quarter, 25¢,
twenty five cents

1093 one dollar, $1.00

1094 five dollars, $5.00

1095 ten dollars, $10.00

1096 first, first place

1097 second, second place

1098 third, third place

1099 fourth, fourth place

1100 fifth, fifth place

ALPHABET
american sign language

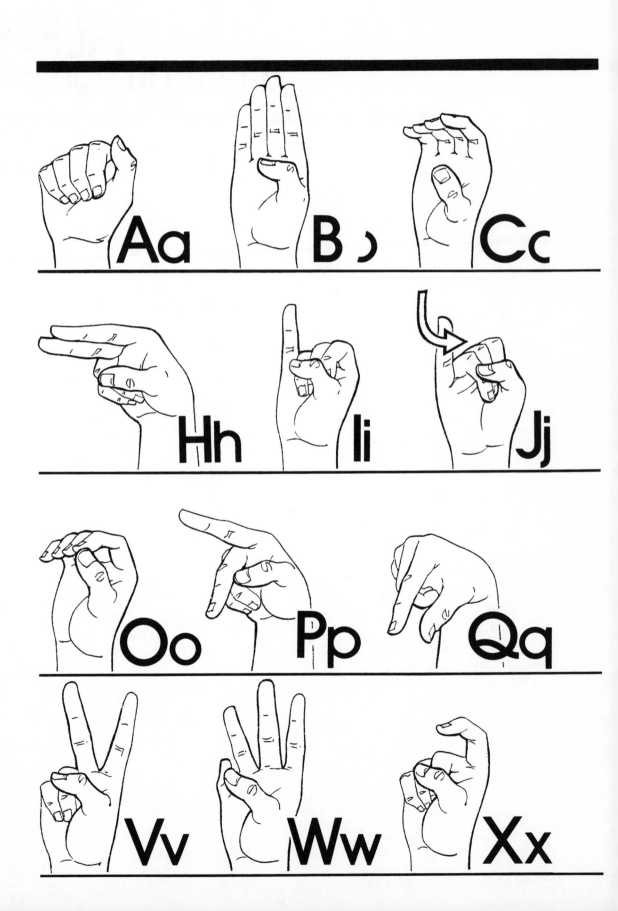

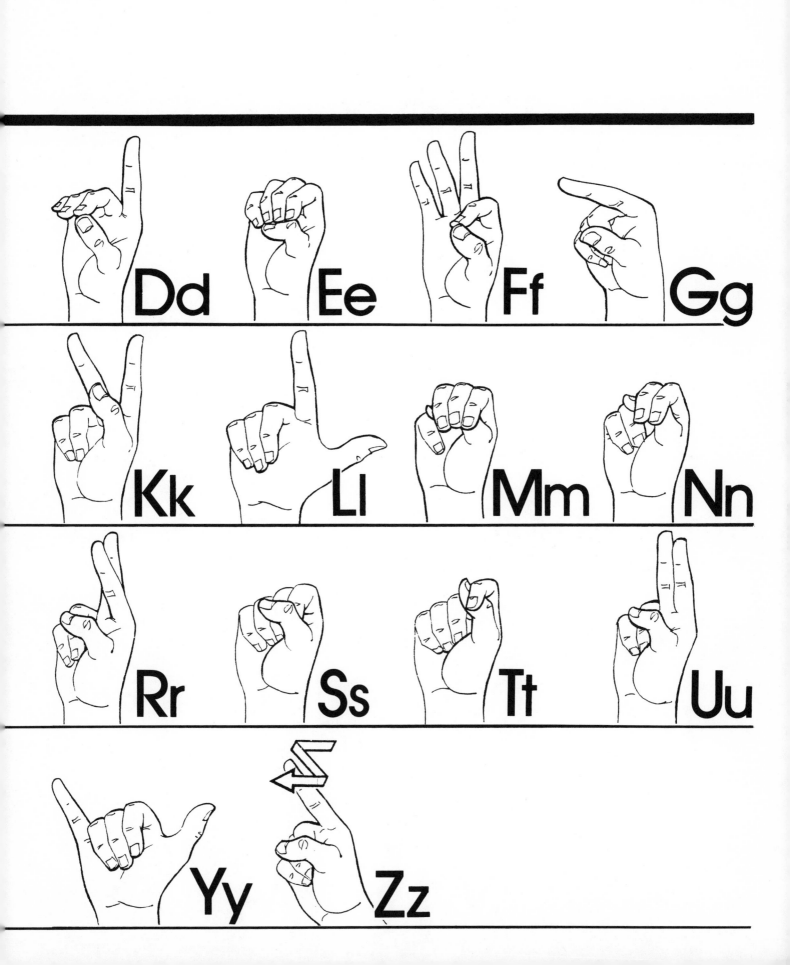

INDEX

For easy location of signs, the illustrations are numbered consecutively. Each number below represents the corresponding number of the illustration in the text. No page numbers are given.